WORD

Made

FLESH

"As a parish priest, my concerns are more practical than anything else: what will bring my people into greater intimacy with the Trinity and help me do the same? Using John Paul II's Theology of the Body, as well as other saints and papal statements, Christopher West has written a little book that can help all enter deeply into the Good News, from priest to high school teen to the woman praying the Rosary. West's comments on scripture are brief, deep, and helpful. The Theology of the Body was written for theologians, while a parish is about the messiness and busyness of average people's lives. Someone needed to bridge the gap, and West has done that with this book on the Sunday readings."

Rev. Ryan Mann
Parochial vicar at St. John Neumann Catholic Church
Strongsville, Ohio

"This new work by Christopher West is an unparalleled gift to preachers and laity alike, providing insightful reflections on the yearly liturgical readings. His expertise in St. John Paul II's Theology of the Body that he brings to bear upon the scriptural texts is such a gift, as he unfolds the mystical depths of the liturgy. As a priest, I'm always trying to figure out how to communicate this glorious, life-transforming vision of love, humanity, and worship in the limited space of a Sunday homily. West's book makes that challenge more attainable; it's a must-have for any priest who desires his people to understand what it means to be invited to the Supper of the Lamb."

Rev. Patrick Schultz
Parochial vicar at Communion of Saints Parish
Cleveland, Ohio

"*Word Made Flesh* is a beautiful guide to the Sunday readings. Christopher West has a gift of making the complex understandable and painting a beautiful picture with his words. Preparing for Sunday Mass with the scripture readings along with these weekly reflections will help draw us closer to the one who wants to marry us, draw us closer to intimacy with him, and who wants us to know the true and beautiful message of our bodies he created. This would make a great gift for so many people."

Suzy Luecke
Pastoral associate at St. Patrick Catholic Church
Cedar Rapids, Iowa

"The more familiar we become with St. John Paul II's Theology of the Body, the more we will benefit from what is arguably his greatest contribution to Catholic life and thought. Christopher West's Word Made Flesh series will help the homilist, as well as the person in the pew, to integrate John Paul's nuptial vision with the scriptures proclaimed at Mass."

Most Rev. Michael J. Sheridan
Bishop of Colorado Springs

"The entirety of the scriptures—from Genesis to Revelation—recounts the story of God's profound love for his creation. Christopher West's *Word Made Flesh* provides an ongoing reflection on this love through the lens of St. John Paul II's catechesis on the nuptial meaning of creation. Since these meditations follow the Sunday Lectionary, every Catholic can benefit from this companion as they pray their way through the liturgical year."

Most Rev. Kevin C. Rhoades
Bishop of Fort Wayne–South Bend

"Christopher West does it again! Through the lens of Theology of the Body, he helps break open the Sunday readings to reveal the deep mysteries of our desires. Let him personally walk alongside you each week and you will find your heart burning within you."

Rose Sweet
Catholic author, speaker, and retreat leader

"Christopher West's new book has been a secret dream of many familiar with Theology of the Body, including myself. So many liturgical Bible readings lend themselves to an explication through the lens of St. John Paul II's masterwork, and now West has connected the dots. As Catholics, we have three sources of Revelation: Creation (the Father), Scripture (the Son), the Church (the Holy Spirit). In *Word Made Flesh*, West, with his gift of clarity, helps us to discern all three sources working together and assists both clergy and laity in breaking open the Word of God in all its physical and spiritual richness and beauty."

Sr. Helena Burns, F.S.P.
Theology of the Body presenter

WORD
Made
FLESH

A Companion to the Sunday Readings
(Cycle A)

Christopher West

AVE MARIA PRESS AVE Notre Dame, Indiana

© 2019 by Christopher West

All rights reserved. No part of this book may be used or reproduced in any manner whatsoever, except in the case of reprints in the context of reviews, without written permission from Ave Maria Press®, Inc., P. O. Box 428, Notre Dame, IN 46556, 1-800-282-1865.

Founded in 1865, Ave Maria Press is a ministry of the United States Province of Holy Cross.

www.avemariapress.com

Paperback: ISBN-13 978-1-59471-935-6

E-book: ISBN-13 978-1-59471-936-3

Cover image © Qweek/iStock.

Cover and text design by Brianna Dombo.

Printed and bound in the United States of America.

ACKNOWLEDGMENTS

My sincere thanks go to Bill Howard, who first proposed the idea of turning my weekly reflections on the Sunday readings into a book. He worked diligently to get this off the ground and bring it to fruition.

Phillip Rolfes and Lindsey Schrock were godsends in all the work they did organizing the manuscript, pulling scripture quotes, and providing scripture references. Thank you!

My thanks also to Ian Rutherford who recommended Ave Maria Press as the right fit for this kind of book.

Finally, my thanks to everyone at Ave Maria Press who embraced this project and brought it to publication.

INTRODUCTION

Christianity is the religion of the "Word"
of God, a word which is "not a written and
mute word, but the Word is incarnate and
living" (St. Bernard). If the Scriptures are
not to remain a dead letter, Christ, the eternal Word of the living God, must, through
the Holy Spirit, "open [our] minds to
understand the Scriptures" (Lk 24:45).
—*Catechism of the Catholic Church*, 108

The sacred words of scripture are, of course, critically
important to our faith. "Still, the Christian faith is not a
'religion of the book,'" as the *Catechism* insists (108). It is the
religion of the Divine Word that "became flesh and made
his dwelling among us" (Jn 1:14). Scripture, in fact, will
remain a dead letter unless every word of it is read in view
of the Word made flesh.

That is the purpose of the volume you now hold in your
hands. Inspired by the scriptural vision St. John Paul II
unfolded for us in his 129 Wednesday audiences from 1979

1

to 1984 that came to be known as the "Theology of the Body" (TOB), the brief, prayerful reflections on the Sunday readings in this book are intended to "open [our] minds to understand the Scriptures" by reading them in light of "the Word [which] is incarnate and living."

ULTIMATE MEANING IS MADE FLESH

Have you ever paused to ponder what the Bible actually means by referring to the eternal Son of God as the Word? "Word" does not quite convey all the richness of the Greek *logos*. "Logos" refers to the rational principle governing the universe—the ultimate meaning, reason, logic, and beauty behind *everything*. And the astounding claim upon which all of Christianity rests is that the human body is God's chosen vehicle for communicating his Word, for communicating ultimate meaning, and for communicating who he is, who we are, and his final plan for the universe.

Just as in Jesus' day, when people hear how important the body is to Christian faith, they often respond as did some of the first disciples: "This saying is hard; who can accept it?" (Jn 6:60). This response is understandable. How could something as earthly as the human body convey something as heavenly as the mystery of God? And yet, if we believe in the meaning of Christmas, we should also believe this claim. For those with eyes to see, our bodies are not only biological; they're theological—they reveal the logic of God; they reveal the ultimate meaning behind everything.

This is why St. John Paul II's Theology of the Body, despite how it is typically framed, is not merely a papal teaching on marital love and human sexuality. It is that, to be sure, but it is also so much more. As John Paul II himself said, what we learn in his TOB "concerns the entire Bible" (TOB 69:8) and plunges us into "the perspective of the whole Gospel, of the whole teaching of the whole mission of Christ" (TOB 49:3). Through the lens of spousal love, John Paul II's Theology of the Body leads to "the rediscovery of the meaning of the whole of existence . . . the meaning of life" (TOB 46:6).

Having spoken since the 1990s to Catholic audiences around the world, it is clear to me that we are often unaware of what is really happening in the liturgy. We "look but do not see and hear but do not listen or understand," as Jesus is quoted saying in Matthew 13:13. Reflecting on the Sunday Mass readings with the help of John Paul II's Theology of the Body is like putting on a pair of glasses that brings the entire biblical story (and the liturgy itself) into focus. Familiar passages and parables suddenly "pop open" enabling us to enter their inner mystery and meaning as never before. We come to see that the whole of the Christian life is an invitation—as Jesus proposed in Matthew 22:1–14 and Luke 14:15–24—to a wedding feast!

GOD WANTS TO MARRY US

Scripture uses many images to help us understand God's love for us. Each image has its own valuable place. But as John Paul II shared, the gift of Christ's body on the Cross gives "definitive prominence to the spousal meaning of God's love" (*Mulieris Dignitatem* 26). In fact, from the beginning to end, the Bible tells a nuptial or marital story. It begins in Genesis with the marriage of the first man and woman, and it ends in Revelation with the marriage of Christ and the Church. Right in the middle of the Bible, we find the erotic poetry of the Song of Songs. These bookends and this centerpiece provide the key for reading and understanding the whole biblical story. Indeed, we can summarize all of sacred scripture with five simple, yet astounding words: *God wants to marry us*. Consider:

> For as a young man marries a virgin,
>   your Builder shall marry you;
> And as the bridegroom rejoices in his bride,
>   so shall your God rejoice in you. (Is 62:5)

> I will betroth you to me forever:
> I will betroth you to me with justice and
>   with judgment
>   with loyalty and with compassion;
> I will betroth you to me with fidelity.
> (Hos 2:19)

God is inviting each of us, in a unique and unrepeatable way, to an unimagined intimacy with him, akin to the intimacy of spouses in one flesh. In fact, as Pope Francis observed, "the very word [used in scripture to describe marital union] . . . 'to cleave' . . . is used to describe our union with God: 'My soul clings to you' (Ps 63:8)." Because of the supreme bliss of union with God, "a love lacking either pleasure or passion is insufficient to symbolize the union of the human heart with God: 'All the mystics have affirmed that supernatural love and heavenly love find the symbols which they seek in marital love'" (*Amoris Laetitia* 13, 142).

While we may need to work through some discomfort or even fear to reclaim the true sacredness, the true holiness of the imagery, the "scandalous" truth is that scripture describes "God's passion for his people using boldly erotic images" as Pope Benedict XVI explained in *Deus Caritas Est* (9). Elsewhere he declared, "*Eros* is part of God's very Heart: the Almighty awaits the 'yes' of his creatures as a young bridegroom that of his bride" (Lenten Message 2007).

We are probably more familiar (and more comfortable) describing God's love as "agape"—the Greek word for sacrificial, self-giving love. Yet God's love "may certainly be called eros," asserted Benedict XVI. In Christ, eros is "supremely ennobled . . . so purified as to become one with agape." Thus, the Bible has no qualms employing the erotic poetry of the Song of Songs as a description of "God's relation to man and man's relation to God." In this way, as Pope Benedict XVI concluded, the Song of Songs became not only an expression of the intimacies of marital love but also "an expression of the essence of biblical faith: that man can indeed enter into union with God—his primordial aspiration" (*Deus Caritas Est* 10).

THE ESSENCE OF BIBLICAL FAITH

Let's try to let this essential message sink in: *the Song of Songs, this unabashed celebration of erotic love, expresses the essence of biblical faith.* How so? The essence of biblical faith is that God came among us in the flesh not only to forgive our sins (as astounding as that gift is); he became "one flesh" with us so we could share in his eternal exchange of love. In the first of his many sermons on the Song of Songs, St. Bernard of Clairvaux aptly described marriage as "the sacrament of endless union with God." The book of Revelation calls this endless union the "marriage of the Lamb" (Rv 19:7).

But there is more. Remember that pithy rhyme we learned as children: "First comes love, then comes marriage, then comes the baby in the baby carriage"? We probably didn't realize as children that we were actually reciting some profound theology. Yes, our bodies tell a divine story; our bodies tell the story that God loves us, wants to marry us, and wants us to "conceive" eternal life within us. This is not merely a metaphor.

Representing all of us, a young Jewish woman named Mary once gave her yes to God's marriage proposal with such totality and fidelity that she literally conceived eternal life in her womb. In a hymn addressed to her, St. Augustine exclaimed, "The Word becomes united with flesh, he makes his covenant with flesh, and your womb is the sacred bed on which this holy union of the Word with flesh is consummated" (Sermon 291). Mary's virginity has always been understood by the Church as the sign of her betrothal to God. She is the "mystic bride of love eternal," as a traditional hymn has it. As such, Mary perfectly fulfills the spousal character of the human vocation in relation to God (see CCC 505).

PENETRATING THE ESSENCE OF THE MYSTERY

In the midst of unfolding the biblical analogy of spousal love, it is very important to understand the bounds within which we are using such language and imagery. "It is obvious," wrote St. John Paul II, "that the analogy of . . . human spousal love, cannot offer an adequate and complete understanding of . . . the divine mystery." God's *"mystery* remains *transcendent with respect to this analogy"* as with respect to any other analogy." At the same time, however, John Paul II maintains that the spousal analogy allows a certain "penetration" into the

very essence of the mystery (see TOB 95b:1). And no biblical author reaches more deeply into this essence than St.
Paul in his letter to the Ephesians.

Quoting directly from Genesis, Paul states:

> For this reason a man shall leave [his]
>   father and [his] mother
>   and be joined to his wife,
> and the two shall become one flesh.

Then, linking the original marriage with the ultimate marriage, he adds, "This is a great mystery, and I mean in reference to Christ and the Church" (Eph 5:31–32).

We can hardly overstate the importance of this passage for St. John Paul II and the whole theological tradition
of the Church. He called it the "summa" ("sum total") of
Christian teaching about who God is and who we are (see
Letter to Families 19). He said that this passage contains the
"crowning" of all the themes in sacred scripture and expresses the "central reality" of the whole of divine revelation (see
TOB 87:3). The mystery spoken of in this passage "is 'great'
indeed," he said. "It is what God . . . wishes above all to
transmit to mankind in his Word." Thus, "one can say that
[this] passage . . . 'reveals—in a particular way—man to
man himself and makes his supreme vocation clear'" (TOB
87:6; 93:2).

So what is this "supreme vocation" we have as human beings that Ephesians 5 makes clear? Stammering for words to describe the ineffable, the mystics call it "nuptial union" . . . with God. Christ is the New Adam who left his Father in heaven. He also left the home of his mother on earth. Why? To mount "the marriage bed of the cross," as St. Augustine portrayed it, unifying himself with the Church and consummating the union forever.

COME TO THE WEDDING FEAST

The more we allow the brilliant rays of St. John Paul II's Theology of the Body to illuminate our vision, the more we come to understand, as the *Catechism* observes, how the "entire Christian life bears the mark of the spousal love of Christ and the Church. Already Baptism, the entry into the People of God, is a nuptial mystery; it is so to speak the nuptial bath which precedes the wedding feast, the Eucharist" (CCC 1617).

I never met my father-in-law; he died when my wife was a young girl. But I admire him tremendously because of the intuition he had as a brand-new husband. At Mass the day after his wedding, having consummated his marriage the night before, he was in tears as he came back to the pew after receiving the Eucharist. When his new bride inquired about his emotional state, he said, "For the first time in my life I understood the meaning of those words, 'This is my body given for you.'"

This was a man for whom the Word of God was not a dead letter. God's Word had become flesh ... *in his own flesh.* This was a man who had been given eyes to see and ears to hear what God's Word is in its very essence: an invitation to a Wedding Feast. My prayer is that this companion to the Sunday readings will help do the same for you.

My hope is that you will keep this little volume with you when you go to Sunday Mass. Use it to guide your prayer after Communion. Or better yet, get to Mass early enough to read the day's readings in advance and then use this companion to help you enter into the treasures of that day's liturgy. Like the disciples on the road to Emmaus, Christ is walking with us to "open the scriptures" to us so as to reveal himself to us in the breaking of the bread. Lord, give us ears that hear and eyes that see. Amen.

THE ADVENT
AND CHRISTMAS
SEASONS

FIRST SUNDAY
OF ADVENT

*Therefore, stay awake! For you do not know on
which day your Lord will come. (Matthew 24:42)*

Advent and the Healing of Desire

The first Sunday of Advent is upon us. In the gospel this
week, Jesus admonishes us to "stay awake" and "be prepared"
for his coming, his advent. Until he comes, people will be
"eating and drinking, marrying and giving in marriage,"
Jesus tells us (Mt 24:38). That's all fine and good. However, there's always a danger of turning our desire for infinite
bliss toward finite pleasures. The pleasures of food, drink,
and marital union, for example, can point the way to the
Infinite, but they're no substitute for it. In short, the challenge of being "awake" and "prepared" for Christ's coming
is the challenge of refusing to take our hungers for God
to things less than God. Hence, St. Paul admonishes the
Romans (and us) to avoid orgies, drunkenness, promiscuity,
and lust. Rather, we should "put on the Lord Jesus Christ
and make no provisions for the desires of the flesh." Here
"desires of the flesh" refer not merely to physical desires but
to those desires that have been misdirected by sin. To "put

on Christ" is to allow grace to redirect our desire *for* God *toward* God. This is the joy of Advent: Christ, the fulfillment of all desire, is coming soon!

Scripture: Isaiah 2:1–5; Psalm 122:1–2, 3–4a, 4b–5, 6–7, 8–9; Romans 13:11–14; Matthew 24:37–44

SECOND SUNDAY OF ADVENT

On that day, the root of Jesse, set up as a signal for the nations, the Gentiles shall seek out, for his dwelling shall be glorious. (Isaiah 11:10)

Hoping and Longing for the Coming of the Kingdom

It's hard to believe the second Sunday of Advent will soon be upon us. In this Sunday's first reading, Isaiah provides a prophecy of what the world will look like when the "kingdom comes." The wolf will be the guest of the lamb. All harm and ruin shall flee. Advent is all about giving ourselves permission to hope and long for that for which we most ardently hope and long: a world of perfect peace and harmony, beginning with peace and harmony *within ourselves*. The first rotten fruit of the Fall, after our rupture with God, was the rupture within ourselves between body and soul. Christ came not only to "save souls" but also to "transform our mortal bodies to conform with his glorified body" (Phil 3:21). And so Isaiah ends with a prophecy of our bodily transformation: "His dwelling shall be glorious." We are that dwelling! "Do you not know that you are the temple of God, and that the Spirit of God dwells in you?" (1 Cor 3:16). John the Baptist proclaims the same in this Sunday's gospel: "He will baptize you with the Holy Spirit and with fire." Let us not fear to be set ablaze!

Scripture: Isaiah 11:1–10; Psalm 72:1–2, 7–8, 12–13, 17; Romans 15:4–9; Matthew 3:1–12

THIRD SUNDAY OF ADVENT

Those whom the Lord ransomed will return and enter Zion singing, crowned with everlasting joy. (Isaiah 35:10a)

The Garden, the Bride, and Everlasting Joy

In this Sunday's first reading, Isaiah describes our redemption using the imagery of a garden: "The steppe will rejoice and bloom . . . with abundant flowers, and rejoice with joyful song." The reading ends with Isaiah's foretelling that the "ransomed will return and enter Zion singing, crowned with everlasting joy." For those with eyes to see, the "spousal key" is unmistakable: the garden, the flowers, the rejoicing, the entering of Zion (an image of the Church-Bride), and the joyful song all point us to the glory of the Song of Songs as we "are a garden enclosed" (Sg 4:12), says the Bridegroom, who longs to "enter Zion." He continues, "Open to me, my sister, my [bride], my dove, my perfect one" (Sg 5:2). And the Bride (Zion-Church) responds, "I opened for my lover" (Sg 5:6). He "has come down to his garden . . . to gather the lilies" (Sg 6:2). Metaphor serves as a proper veil honoring the intimacy of the spousal mystery. Let us be delicate and reverent. But let us also "be strong" and "fear not," as Isaiah urges, to enter the mystery of Christ's nuptial union with the Church (with us!). Therein lies the "everlasting joy" Isaiah proclaims!

Scripture: Isaiah 35:1–6a, 10; Psalm 146:6–7, 8–9a, 9b–10; James 5:7–10; Matthew 11:2–11

FOURTH SUNDAY
OF ADVENT

*When his mother Mary was betrothed to Joseph,
but before they lived together, she was found with child
through the Holy Spirit. (Matthew 1:18)*

She Was Found with Child
through the Holy Spirit

In this Sunday's readings, Isaiah prophesies that "the virgin shall conceive and bear a son." St. Paul proclaims Christ "descended from David according to the flesh, but established as the Son of God . . . according to the Spirit." Matthew tells us that Mary "was found with child through the Holy Spirit." Mary's virginal conception of Christ—far from being a negation of sexuality as is often presumed—points to the ultimate purpose and meaning of sexuality, which is to point us to union with God. He made us male and female and called the two to nuptial union as a sacramental sign of a much, much greater reality. The ultimate nuptial union, says St. Augustine, "is between the word and the flesh and the bridal chamber of the union is the virgin's womb." As St. John Paul II wrote, "God's nuptial love, announced by the prophets, is concentrated on [Mary] perfectly and definitively. She is also the virgin-bride to whom it is granted conceiving and bearing the Son of God: *the particular fruit of the nuptial love of God toward humanity*, represented and almost comprehended in Mary." We, too, are called in an analogous way to "open" our humanity to these divine nuptials as the psalmist proclaims: "Let the Lord enter; he is the king of glory."

Scripture: Isaiah 7:10–14; Psalm 24:1–2, 3–4, 5–6; Romans 1:1–7; Matthew 1:18–24

THE NATIVITY OF THE LORD (CHRISTMAS)

For a child is born to us, a son is given to us;
upon his shoulder dominion rests. (Isaiah 9:5a)

Christmas Fills Us with Wonder at the Mystery of the Woman's Body

There is a constant proclamation of a fundamental truth throughout the Christmas season that is essential but often overlooked: *God comes to us through woman's body!* "For a child is born to us, a son is given us," proclaims Isaiah in the

Midnight Mass readings for Christmas. And in the gospel the angel announces that "a savior has been born for you who is Christ the Lord." To recognize woman's body as the "portal" through which Eternity enters time, through which the Infinite enters the finite so we can be taken into Eternity, into Infinity; to recognize this is to be filled with awe and wonder at the mystery of woman. It is to be filled with the "spiritually mature fascination" St. John Paul II spoke of in his Theology of the Body. It's a holy fascination in woman's "mystery" that untwists the distorted fascination so prevalent in our world today. "The Bible (and subsequently the liturgy) honors and praises throughout the centuries 'the womb that carried you and the breasts that you sucked' (Lk 11:27). These words are a eulogy of motherhood, of femininity, of the feminine body in its typical expression of creative love" (TOB 21:5). These words, prayerfully pondered, will take us into the glory of the mystery and gift of Christmas.

Scripture (Mass at Midnight): Isaiah 9:1–6; Psalm 96:1–2a, 2b–3, 11–12, 13; Titus 2:11–14; Luke 2:1–14

THE HOLY FAMILY OF JESUS, MARY AND JOSEPH

And let the peace of Christ control your hearts, the
peace into which you were also called as one body.
(Colossians 3:15)

The Love That Brings Peace

The first thing that Christ said to his disciples in the upper room after his Resurrection is "Peace be with you." Christ came for this purpose: that we might have his peace, which is to say, that we might rest in the love of the Father as he does. As the *Catechism* says, "The personal relation of the Son to the Father is something that man cannot conceive of nor the angelic powers even dimly see: and yet, the Spirit of the Son grants a participation in that very relation to us who believe that Jesus is the Christ and that we are born of God"(CCC 2780). Notice the familial terms: son, father, born. The family is born when husband and wife become "one body." And we are called into God's family (God's peace) inasmuch as we become "one body" with Christ in the sacraments of Baptism and Eucharist. When the peace of loving divinely "controls our hearts," we needn't fear admonitions such as "Wives, be subordinate to your husbands, as is proper in the Lord" (Col 3:18). For what is "proper in the Lord" is not a relationship of servitude ("it shall not be so among you," Mt 20:26), but a relationship of love: "Husbands, love your wives" (Col 3:19). And the Apostle clarifies what he means more specifically in Ephesians 5:25: "Husbands, love your wives as Christ loved the Church." Doesn't every woman want to be loved in this way? This peace-giving love is precisely the love exemplified in the Holy Family.

Scripture: Sirach 3:2–7, 12–14; Psalm 128:1–2, 3, 4–5; Colossians 3:12–21 (longer form) or Colossians 3:12–17 (shorter form); Matthew 2:13–15, 19–23

THE OCTAVE DAY/ SOLEMNITY OF THE BLESSED VIRGIN MARY, MOTHER OF GOD

When the fullness of time had come, God sent his Son,
born of a woman. (Galatians 4:4)

God Sent His Son, Born of a Woman

St. Paul proclaims in the second reading that "God sent his Son, born of a woman." At the moment the Eternal Son of God was conceived in Mary's womb, he became *matter* and she became *mater* (the Latin term for "mother"). And her *mater*-hood, in turn, reinstated the ultimate truth of matter. In God's loving design, matter is the proper form, the proper vehicle, the proper "sacrament" of divine love. But since the dawn of sin, matter has resisted divine love's incarnation, often violently so. Who, then, is this *woman?* "Who is this who comes forth like the dawn, beautiful as the white moon, pure as the blazing sun, fearsome as the celestial visions?" (Sg 6:10). She is the one who freely opened matter to love's *incarnation*, thus becoming *Mater* of God. Today, on the Solemnity of the Blessed Virgin Mary, Mother of God, keep in mind that with the war on gender, humanity wants to ascend above and beyond the body, as if matter didn't matter. But this is humanity trying to be "like God." Mary's motherhood proclaims the astonishing truth that *God wants to be like us.* God descends deeply into flesh, into Mary's flesh. Mary's *mater*-hood proclaims to the whole world: matter matters!

Scripture: Numbers 6:22–27; Psalm 67:2–3, 5, 6, 8; Galatians 4:4–7; Luke 2:16–21

SECOND SUNDAY
AFTER CHRISTMAS

And the Word became flesh and made his dwelling among us.
(John 1:14)

Regenerated by the Father unto Eternal Life

In today's second reading, St. Paul writes that God had a plan for us "before the foundation of the world." He speaks of the "hope that belongs to his call" and the "riches of glory" that we are meant to inherit (Ephesians 1:4, 18). What is this plan and this hope? What are these riches? Today's gospel answers these questions: to those who accepted the invitation, "he gave power to become children of God . . . born not by natural generation . . . but of God" (Jn 1:12–13). We are all generated by the union of our father and mother. This is the natural reality. But this is just a shadow of the plan God had for us before the foundation of the world. From eternity, God has desired to expand participation in the ecstasy and bliss of his own Trinitarin Love—by inviting us to be part of it! This is why we exist: to participate not only in natural life, but in the divine life of the Trinity. As St. John says, "What came to be through him was life, and this life was the light of the human race"

(Jn 1:4). In other words, the divine life shining with glorious brilliance in Christ's humanity ("the Word became flesh") is what illuminates the meaning, purpose, and desitiny of our humanity. This is the hope that belongs to his call: we are destined to participate in all the riches of God's glory. How? After the pattern of Christ's Incarnation, we are called to be regenerated by the Father, through the power of the Holy Spirit, in the womb of Mary, our mother. This is what happens in Baptism: we are regenerated through the mystical nuptials of Christ and the Church. And our bodies proclaim this "great mystery" (see Ephesians 5:31–32).

Scripture: Sirach 24:1–2, 8–12; Psalm 147:12–13, 14–15, 19–20; Ephesians 1:3–6, 15–18; John 1:1–18 (longer form) or John 1:1–5, 9–14 (shorter form)

EPIPHANY OF THE LORD

Rise up in splendor, Jerusalem! Your light has come, the glory of the Lord shines upon you. (Isaiah 60:1)

The Sons and Daughters of Jerusalem Come from Afar

Each of this Sunday's readings celebrates the Epiphany of the Lord to the Gentiles. In the gospel account of the visit of the magi from the East, we discover that the Christ child is not only the Savior of the Jews but also the Savior of the world. St. Paul affirms this in the second reading that "the Gentiles are coheirs, members of the same body." And the first reading tells us that Jerusalem has sons and daughters that come "from afar." In what sense does Jerusalem bear sons and daughters? Ah, in the spousal mystery of the scriptures, the mystery of Jerusalem (God's holy city and dwelling place) is fulfilled in Mary who is both the Mother of God and "the Mother of all the living." Enter the first reading from this perspective and the mystery opens to us: "Rise up in splendor, [Mary] ... the glory of the Lord shines upon you." While darkness covers the rest of the earth, and "thick clouds cover the peoples," the Lord shines on Mary, and over her "appears his glory." This woman brings God to earth, her body revealing the glory of the Lord to all the kings and nations of the world. If we, like the wise men, set out on a journey of discovery, we "shall be radiant" at what we see and our "heart shall throb and overflow." Mary, show us the glory of your Son!

Scripture: Isaiah 60:1–6; Psalm 72:1–2, 7–8, 10–11, 12–13; Ephesians 3:2–3a, 5–6; Matthew 2:1–12

BAPTISM OF THE LORD

Heaven was opened and the Holy Spirit descended upon him in bodily form like a dove. (Luke 3:21–22)

Christ Makes Baptism a Bath of Rebirth

Today we celebrate the Lord's baptism in the River Jordan. It is a mystery of unfathomable depths—in fact, as the *Catechism* tells us, it is a "nuptial mystery" (CCC 1617). In the second reading, St. Paul speaks of the "generous love of God" that "saved us through the bath of rebirth and renewal by the Holy Spirit." A *generous* love, as the root of the word indicates, is a love that *generates*, that is, a love that gives birth. The Holy Spirit—"the Lord, the giver of life," as we say in the Nicene Creed—is the generous/generating love of God. Natural generation through perishable seed points to the supernatural generation of Baptism in which Christ gives his "imperishable seed" (CCC 1228) to his Church-Bride. She then "brings forth sons [and daughters] . . . to a new and immortal life" (CCC 507). In Baptism we encounter an open exchange between heaven and earth: heaven opens its mysteries to be poured out on earth, and earth opens to receive them. *This* is what occurred in Christ's baptism: "Heaven was opened and the Holy Spirit descended," as we read in the gospel. In turn, earth opened and all her waters were impregnated with the power to give new life. Blessed are those who are regenerated through water and the Holy Spirit. Lord, help us understand how blessed we are.

Scripture: Isaiah 40:1–5, 9–11 (or Isaiah 42:1–4, 6–7); Psalm 104:1b–2, 3–4, 24–25, 27–28, 29–30 (or Psalm 29:1–2, 3–4, 3, 9–10); Titus 2:11–14; 3:4–7 (or Acts 10:34–38); Luke 3:15–16, 21–22

ORDINARY TIME

SECOND SUNDAY IN ORDINARY TIME

*Behold, the Lamb of God, who takes away
the sin of the world. (John 1:29)*

The Love of the Bridegroom for His Bride

How would John the Baptist's proclamation of Christ as "the Lamb of God" (Jn 1:29) have sounded to his Jewish audience? Lambs were animals ritually sacrificed to God. They were *slain*. Christ is the Lamb who has been "slain from the foundation of the world" (Rv 13:8). The love revealed in Christ's sacrifice on the Cross is eternal: beyond time but poured out in time to reach us *here and now*. And this eternal love that has pierced through the time barrier to reach our concrete, time-bound lives is the love of the Bridegroom for his Bride. The sacrifice of "the Lamb" consummates the "marriage of the Lamb" (Rv 19:7). As St. Augustine put it, Christ "came to the marriage bed of the cross, a bed not of pleasure, but of pain, united himself with the woman [his Bride, the Church], and consummated the union forever." All of this nuptial potency is contained in the words of John the Baptist—the best man who stands by the Bridegroom (see John 3:29) when he says in awe, "Behold, the Lamb of God."

Scripture: Isaiah 49:3, 5–6; Psalm 40:2, 4, 7–8, 8–9, 10; 1 Corinthians 1:1–3; John 1:29–34

THIRD SUNDAY IN ORDINARY TIME

One thing I ask of the Lord; this I seek:
To dwell in the house of the Lord all the days of my life,
That I may gaze on the loveliness of the Lord
and contemplate his temple. (Psalm 27:4)

The Body Reveals the Loveliness of the Lord

"One thing I ask of the Lord; this I seek . . . that I may gaze on the loveliness of the Lord and contemplate his temple." The thesis statement of St. John Paul II's Theology of the Body beautifully illuminates this Sunday's psalm: "The body . . . was created to transfer into the visible reality of the world the mystery hidden from eternity in God, and thus be a sign of it" (TOB 19:4). Our bodies are that temple (see 1 Corinthians 6:19). And it is by contemplating them with purity of heart that we come to "gaze on the loveliness of the Lord." For purity, as John Paul II taught us, "is the glory of God in the human body" (TOB 57:3). "Blessed are the clean of heart, for they will see God" (Mt 5:8). If we desire to "see God," to "gaze upon his loveliness," we must be willing to pass through some very painful fires of purification. It can be a daily struggle. Slowly, but surely, as we walk through those "fires," we come to see the human body—in all its glory as male and female—as a sign of the Lord's loveliness.

Scripture: Isaiah 8:23b–9:3; Psalm 27:1, 4, 13–14; 1 Corinthians 1:10–13, 17; Matthew 4:12–23

FOURTH SUNDAY IN ORDINARY TIME

Blessed are the poor in spirit, for theirs is the kingdom of heaven. (Matthew 5:3)

Opening Our Poverty to God's Riches

We repeat this passage several times as the response to today's psalm and we encounter it yet again in the gospel, at the start of the beatitudes. It must be important! Everyone is poor before God. But the "poor in spirit" are those who realize and humbly accept their poverty, confident that God desires to fill it with his riches. As finite creatures, our poverty is the only thing that approaches something infinite. Our infinite poverty, in fact, is like a reverse image of God's infinite richness. It's the "chalice" into which he can pour his infinite love. This is why the Church is always feminine, she's always the Bride, and God is always the Bridegroom. It can't be the other way around. The Bridegroom is the one who *fills* and the Bride is the one who is *filled*. To be empty, needy, weak, and open: this is just where we need to be if we want to inherit the Kingdom. This is foolishness, however, to a world where survival of the fittest, self-sufficiency, and self-glorification are the name of the game. But soon and very soon we will all face the reckoning of which St. Paul speaks in the second reading: "God chose the foolish of the world to shame the wise, and God chose the weak of the world to shame the strong, and God chose the lowly and despised of the world, those who count for nothing, to reduce to nothing those who are something, so that no human being might boast before God" (1 Cor 1:27–29). If we are to boast, let us boast only in our weakness (see 2 Cor 12:9).

Scripture: Zephaniah 2:3; 3:12–13; Psalm 146:6c–7, 8–9a, 9b–10; 1 Corinthians 1:26–31; Matthew 5:1–12a

FIFTH SUNDAY IN ORDINARY TIME

Share your bread with the hungry,
shelter the oppressed and the homeless;
clothe the naked when you see them, and do not
turn your back on your own. (Isaiah 58:7)

Mercy for Our Own Bodies and for Every Body

The words of the first reading command us to take the corporal works of mercy seriously. (The corporal works of mercy are feed the hungry, give drink to the thirsty, clothe the naked, shelter the homeless, visit the sick, visit the imprisoned, and bury the dead.) Corporal, from the Latin word *corpus*, means "of or relating to the human body." The Latin word for mercy, *misericordia*, means "a heart that gives itself to those in misery." Our hemorrhaging world is crying out for this merciful love. The need couldn't be more urgent: we live in a veritable wasteland of human misery and woundedness because of our failure to understand the meaning of our bodies. We must not fear to throw our wounded selves wide open to Christ, to invite his healing, merciful love to come into all the diseased images we have of our bodies and our sexuality, so that he can touch our wounds and transform us into the men and women we are truly created to be. For such a time as this have we been given St. John Paul II's Theology of the Body. Take up a study of it, and let Christ's mercy ever more deeply into your own wounded humanity so you can become a living witness of corporal mercy to others. When we practice the corporal works of mercy, the Lord promises, among other things, that our wounds "shall quickly be healed."

Scripture: Isaiah 58:7–10; Psalm 112:4–5, 6–7, 8–9; 1 Corinthians 2:1–5; Matthew 5:13–16

SIXTH SUNDAY IN ORDINARY TIME

I tell you, unless your righteousness surpasses that of the scribes and Pharisees, you will not enter the kingdom of heaven. (Matthew 5:20)

The Spirit Gives New Form to Our Desires

What would Jesus' declaration about righteousness have sounded like to the Jews who first heard it? The scribes and the Pharisees were considered the most righteous of all. The problem was, in St. John Paul II's language, while they conformed to the ethic, their ethos was far from God. An *ethic* is an external norm or rule. *Ethos* refers to a person's inner world of values, what attracts and repulses us deep in the heart. In the Sermon on the Mount, Christ is not only confirming God's ethical code; he is calling us to a new ethos. We could read Christ's words about adultery, for example, as follows: "You've heard the ethic not to commit adultery, but the problem is your *ethos* is off: you desire to commit adultery." So what are we supposed to do? This is precisely where the gospel becomes the Good News: We are not left to our own flaws, weaknesses, and sinfulness. In the "Sermon on the Mount . . . the Spirit of the Lord gives new form to our desires, those inner movements that animate our lives" (CCC 2764). Come, Holy Spirit! Come give new form to our desires!

Scripture: Sirach 15:15–20; Psalm 119:1–2, 4–5, 17–18, 33–34; 1 Corinthians 2:6–10; Matthew 5:17–37

SEVENTH SUNDAY IN ORDINARY TIME

But I say to you, love your enemies and pray for those who persecute you. (Matthew 5:44)

Lord, Save Us from Self-Reliance!

This Sunday's readings offer challenging directions for our lives. In the first reading, God commands us, "Be holy, for I, the Lord, your God, am holy." And in the gospel, Jesus says we have to love even our enemies. Our response is usually one of being willing but not so able to follow through. The problem is that if all we have heard is *what* we're called to without hearing *how* we're called to it, we still have yet to hear the *good news* of this gospel. As St. John Paul II boldly proclaims in *Veritatis Splendor*, "Love and life according to the Gospel cannot be thought of first and foremost as a kind of precept, because what they demand is beyond man's abilities. They are possible only as a result of a gift of God who heals, restores, and transforms the human heart by his grace." Living the Gospel, then, according to John Paul II, is "*a possibility opened to man exclusively by grace*, by the gift of God, by his love." At times the demands of the Gospel can feel incredibly burdensome. And yet, Jesus insists that "my yoke is easy, and my burden light" (Mt 11:30). Likewise, St. John insists that God's "commandments are not burdensome" (1 Jn 5:3). If they *feel* burdensome, chances are we are relying on our own strength to carry them out. Lord, forgive us of the sin of self-reliance. Teach us to rely on you.

Scripture: Leviticus 19:1–2, 17–18; Psalm 103:1–2, 3–4, 8, 10, 12–13; 1 Corinthians 3:16–23; Matthew 5:38–48

EIGHTH SUNDAY IN ORDINARY TIME

*Learn from the way the wild flowers grow.
They do not work or spin. But I tell you that
not even Solomon in all his splendor was
clothed like one of them. (Matthew 6:28b–29)*

How We Learn to Trust God from the Flowers

When Jesus says, "Learn from the way the wild flowers grow," what mystery might he be inviting us into with these words? Why are we so attracted to flowers? Why do we love to see them, smell them, and display them everywhere, especially in our homes and our churches? Why does a bride carry them down a petal-strewn aisle on the way to meet her bridegroom? We may answer, "Because they're beautiful of course." Yes, they are. But *why* are flowers so beautiful? What *is* a flower? To put it plainly, a flower is one of nature's most beautiful reproductive organs, opened before the loving heat of the sun, so that, to quote the Song of Songs, its fragrance might be "spread abroad" (Sg 4:16). And that luscious fragrance is "spread abroad" for one purpose: to attract "lovers" (pollinators). This is how "the wild flowers grow." What can we learn about trusting God from wildflowers? Sirach reminds us to "open up your petals, like roses" (Sir 39:13). The Blessed Virgin Mary is the "mystical rose" because she is the flower who opens before the love and providence of God. May Mary, the most wild flower of all, teach us how to open and to trust.

Scripture: Isaiah 49:14–15; Psalm 62:2–3, 6–7, 8–9; 1 Corinthians 4:1–5; Matthew 6:24–34

THE LENT AND
EASTER SEASONS

FIRST SUNDAY OF LENT

*Jesus was led by the Spirit into the desert
to be tempted by the devil. (Matthew 4:1)*

Overcoming Temptation through Trust

All of the temptations we face are rooted in the original temptation of Adam. "There is only one temptation," as Msgr. Lorenzo Albacete put it. This original or primordial temptation "is the temptation to believe that the fulfillment of the desires of the human heart depends entirely on us." By asking man and woman not to *take* the fruit, God was inviting us into a relationship of trust. As we read in Psalm 81, "'I am the LORD your God. . . . Open wide your mouth that I may fill it. . . .' But my people did not listen to my words. . . . So I thrust them away to the hardness of their heart; 'Let them walk in their own [designs]'" (Ps 81:11–13). That's sin at its root: We don't trust in God's designs, so we choose to follow our own desires. And the very first thing to suffer due to Adam's disobedience was the sexual relationship. Lust enters the world. Shame enters the world. And later in human history, Christ enters to redeem our shame, to restore the possibility of love. How? By trusting in his hunger that the Father would fulfill the desires of his heart. Jesus, teach us how to trust.

Scripture: Genesis 2:7–9, 3:1–7; Psalm 51:3–4, 5–6, 12–13, 17; Romans 5:12–19; Matthew 4:1–11

SECOND SUNDAY OF LENT

He saved us and called us to a holy life,
not according to our works but according to
his own design and the grace bestowed on us
in Christ Jesus before time began. (2 Timothy 1:9)

Bodies Ablaze with Divine Glory

The Father's plan to bestow eternal life on us in Christ is a plan from all eternity. It's not simply the result of the Fall. We are reminded of this in this Sunday's second reading. St. Paul tells Timothy of "the grace bestowed on us in Christ Jesus before time began." God has *always* wanted a Bride for his Son. He has always wanted human flesh to participate in the life of the Trinity through the marriage of Christ and the Church. This eternal marital plan is "now made manifest through the appearance of our savior Christ Jesus, who destroyed death and brought life and immortality to light through the gospel." What does human flesh participating in eternal life and immortality look like? Peter, James, and John caught a glimpse of it when, as reported in this Sunday's gospel, they climbed "a high mountain" with Jesus and saw his body *participating in* and *revealing* the life of the Trinity. This is the ultimate truth to which the Gospel leads us: *bodily* participation in divine glory. Christianity is always the Gospel of the body. This is our faith. And so in the closing prayer of Mass, we pray to "keep faithful" to this gospel so that we "may always desire and at last attain that glory whose beauty [Christ] showed in his own Body, to the amazement of his Apostles." Peter, James, and John, pray for us.

Scripture: Genesis 12:1–4a; Psalm 33:4–5, 18–19, 20, 22; 2 Timothy 1:8b–10; Matthew 17:1–9

THIRD SUNDAY OF LENT

If you knew the gift of God and who is saying to you, "Give me a drink," you would have asked him and he would have given you living water. (John 4:10)

Jesus Is the Perfect Lover

In the first reading, the Israelites grumble against Moses for leading them into the desert to die of thirst. In the second reading, St. Paul tells us that "the love of God has been poured into our hearts through the Holy Spirit." And in the gospel account of the woman at the well, the two readings come together: Jesus uses the woman's physical thirst to point her to her deeper spiritual thirst for love. "Go call your husband," says Jesus, gently pointing out that the woman had taken her deep thirst for love to various sexual relationships. She had, in fact, been with six men (six being the imperfect biblical number). Jesus, in a supreme act of tenderness and mercy, comes to her as her "seventh lover." Seven is the perfect biblical number. In his dialogue with her, it's as if he were saying, "I know you are thirsty for love, I know. But, my beloved, you've been looking for love in the wrong places. I am the love you've been looking for!" In Jesus' words from the gospel, "If you knew the gift of God and who is saying to you 'Give me a drink,' you would have asked him and he would have given you living water. . . . Whoever drinks the water I shall give will never thirst; the water I shall give will become in him a spring of water welling up to eternal life." This is the hope, St. Paul writes, that "does not disappoint."

Scripture: Exodus 17:3–7; Psalm 95:1–2, 6–7, 8–9; Romans 5:1–2, 5–8; John 4:5–42

FOURTH SUNDAY OF LENT

He spat on the ground and made clay with the saliva,
and smeared the clay on his eyes, and said to him,
"Go wash in the Pool of Siloam." (John 9:6–7a)

Jesus Heals Us with His Saliva

In this Sunday's gospel, we hear in great detail how Jesus gave sight to a blind man. Jesus "spat on the ground and made clay with the saliva, and smeared the clay on his eyes." Spat. Ground. Clay. Saliva. Smeared. It's all so visceral. So earthy. And let's be honest: it can seem, well, kinda *gross*. Bodily fluids often make us very uneasy. Ew! Yuck! Ick! Nasty! Jesus was spat upon as an insult. But Jesus' spit smeared on the blind man was a way of expressing his profound love for this man. All of this is *literally* true, though we don't really like to think about such details. But every detail of the gospel is there for a reason, and we would do well to think about them. Here's something else worth pondering: lovers don't recoil when they exchange bodily fluids. They actually *desire* to do so. Spousal love removes the "ick factor." The body (and its fluids) is meant to express the language of spousal love. Jesus' body (and its fluids, especially his blood) is the ultimate expression of this. If we recoil at the thought of such intimacy with Jesus, we will not know the depths of his love. And we'll remain blind. Jesus, smear your saliva-clay on our eyes and heal us of our blindness!

Scripture: 1 Samuel 16:1b, 6–7, 10–13a; Psalm 23:1–3a, 3b–4, 5, 6; Ephesians 5:8–14; John 9:1–41

FIFTH SUNDAY
OF LENT

I will open your graves and have you rise from them.
(Ezekiel 37:12)

The Stench of Death and the Fragrance of Glory

This Sunday's readings are all about the resurrection of the body. The Lord proclaims through Ezekiel, "I will open your graves and have you rise from them" (Ez 37:12). The psalm response assures us: "With the Lord there is mercy and fullness of redemption." This "fullness of redemption," we must remember, is not only the redemption of our souls but also always includes "the redemption of our bodies" (Rom 8:23). Do not confuse St. Paul's sharp words in the second reading about "the flesh" with a disparagement of the body. "Flesh" here means the whole human being cut off from God's Spirit. But if we open our whole body-soul personality to God's Spirit, Paul assures us that "the one who raised Christ from the dead will give life to your mortal bodies also" (Rom 8:11). We see this powerfully foreshadowed in the resurrection of Lazarus. When Jesus told the bystanders to take away the stone, Martha retorted, "Lord, by now there will be a stench." Jesus: "Didn't I tell you that if you believe you will see the glory of God?" Believe what? That Christ himself is "the resurrection and the life"? That Christ's love can transform the stench of our rotting flesh into fragrance of his glory? When we believe in his love, we happily "expose our stench." When we don't, we hide it behind stones. Lord, give us the courage to remove the stones in our lives that keep us from seeing your glory.

Scripture: Ezekiel 37:12–14; Psalm 130:1–2, 3–4, 5–6, 7–8; Romans 8:8–11; John 11:1–45

PALM SUNDAY OF THE LORD'S PASSION

Christ Jesus, though he was in the form of God, did not regard equality with God something to be grasped. (Philippians 2:6)

Am I Grasping at Divine Life?

We all stand before God with one of two postures: *grasping* or *receptivity*. The deepest desire of the human heart is to share in God's life. The good news is that the deepest desire of God's heart is to share his life with us: as the *Catechism of the Catholic Church* says, the "Son of God became man so that we might become God" (460), so that we might participate in the divine nature (see 2 Peter 1:4). If this is true, then fulfillment of our deepest ache and longing comes not from grasping at divine life (and making ourselves "like God") but from remaining—come what may—in a posture of trusting receptivity before the promise of God. This is Christ's posture on the Cross. Though he *was* God, he did not deem equality with God something to be *grasped*. Here, quoting an expression of St. Paul VI, we see the "religion of the God who became man" encountering "the religion (for such it is) of man who makes himself God."

Scripture: (At the Procession) Matthew 21:1–11; (At Mass) Isaiah 50:4–7; Psalm 22:8–9, 17–18, 19–20, 23–24; Philippians 2:6–11; Matthew 26:14–27, 66

THE RESURRECTION OF THE LORD

When Simon Peter arrived after him, he went into the tomb and saw the burial cloths there, and the cloth that had covered his head. (John 20:6b–7a)

Escaping the Bonds of Death and Corruption

In Easter Sunday's gospel reading, Peter and the "other disciple whom Jesus loved" arrived at the tomb and "saw the burial cloths." Recall that when Jesus raised Lazarus from the dead, someone had to untie Lazarus from his burial cloths. But Christ's Resurrection takes the human body to a realm beyond the resurrection of Lazarus, who later died again. As the *Catechism of the Catholic Church* teaches, the fact that Christ's burial cloths were left behind signifies that "Christ's body had escaped the bonds of death and corruption" (657). Astounding! Perhaps we've heard it too many times for it to affect us. Ask for new ears to hear this proclamation: Christ's body has indeed escaped the bonds of death and corruption. And here's the good part for us: we have been invited into the same glory of life beyond death! As St. Paul writes in the Letter to the Colossians, "For you have died, and your life is hidden with Christ in God. When Christ your life appears, then you too will appear with him in glory." Lord, help us enter in.

Scripture: Acts 10:34a, 37–43; Psalm 118:1–2, 16–17, 22–23; Colossians 3:1–4 (or 1 Corinthians 5:6b–8); John 20:1–9 (or Matthew 28:1–10)

SECOND SUNDAY OF EASTER/SUNDAY OF DIVINE MERCY

Blessed be the God and Father of our Lord
Jesus Christ, who in his great mercy gave us
a new birth to a living hope through the resurrection
of Jesus Christ from the dead. (1 Peter 1:3)

New Birth through the Womb of Mercy

On the second Sunday of Easter we celebrate Divine Mercy Sunday, named by St. John Paul II to promote the visions of St. Faustina Kowalska and to reflect on how God's mercy can overcome sin. The First Letter of Peter tells us that God "in his great mercy gave us a new birth to a living hope through the resurrection of Jesus Christ." When we read scripture with spousal lenses, verses like this leap out at us. One of the Hebrew words often translated into English as "compassion" or "mercy" originally referred to a woman's womb. We are given new birth through God's mercy precisely through the waters of Baptism. And Baptism, John Paul II tells us, is "the expression of spousal love" (TOB 91:7). When Christ's spousal love is poured out in the

Sacrament of Baptism, his Church-Bride "brings forth sons, who are conceived by the Holy Spirit and born of God, to a new and immortal life" (CCC 507). This is a *virginal* birth, of course, by grace. Nonetheless, there is a certain analogy between the two orders (nature and grace). Since grace builds on nature, the natural way of conception and birth serves in some way as the model of supernatural conception and birth. How are we naturally begotten? Through the union of man and woman. How are we supernaturally begotten? Through the union of Christ and the Church. This new inheritance grants us the salvation that, as St. Peter tells us, is the goal of our faith.

Scripture: Acts 2:42–47; Psalm 118:2–4, 13–15, 22–24; 1 Peter 1:3–9; John 20:19–31

THIRD SUNDAY OF EASTER

Jesus himself drew near and walked with them,
but their eyes were prevented from recognizing him.
(Luke 24:15b–16)

Jesus Opens Our Eyes to the Truth of His Body

Something is mysteriously different about Jesus' body after the Resurrection. The disciples walking with Jesus to Emmaus could see him, but they couldn't really *see* him: "Jesus himself drew near and walked with them, but their eyes were prevented from recognizing him." He was only later "made known to them in the breaking of the bread." At that moment, as Pope Benedict XVI put it, the disciples "experience in reverse fashion what happened to Adam and Eve when they ate the fruit of the tree of the knowledge of good and evil: their eyes are opened." When Genesis reports that Adam and Eve's eyes were "opened" (see Genesis 3:7), the truth is precisely the reverse: they became blind. Prior to Original Sin, man and woman *saw* the mystery of God revealed through their bodies—the mystery of life-giving love and communion was literally inscribed by God in their sexuality. Shame is the fruit of seeing the body without *seeing* the body, without recognizing God's mystery in the body. Entering into the power of the Eucharist is what heals our blindness. Here, Christ the Bridegroom offers his body in life-giving love for his Bride. Communion is restored, and we come to *see* the divine mystery in and through the body. Jesus, draw near and walk with us. Open the scriptures to us. And open our eyes!

Scripture: Acts 2:14, 22–33; Psalm 16:1–2a, 5, 7–8, 9–10, 11; 1 Peter 1:17–21; Luke 24:13–35

FOURTH SUNDAY OF EASTER

I came so that they might have life and have it more abundantly. (John 10:10b)

Jesus Is Bridegroom and Life-Giver

Christ is the Bridegroom of the Church, and precisely as a Bridegroom, he is a creator, a *life-giver*. Easter is celebrated in the spring for a reason. All of creation is singing the song of new life. All of creation is telling the story of Easter, of God the life-giver. And the life-giving mystery inscribed in the natural world culminates in us, in our creation as male and female and the call of the two to "be fertile and multiply" (Gn 1:28). Our bodies tell the story of God's eternal plan to marry us and fill us with eternal life. Here, also, is where the thief "comes only to steal and slaughter and destroy." Our sexuality, precisely because it reveals the "great mystery" of Christ's life-giving love for the Church (see Ephesians 5:31–32), puts us at the center of a great battle between good and evil, love and sin, and life and death, a battle we see all around us today. The First Letter of Peter reminds us that Christ "himself bore our sins in his body on the cross" so that we might be "free from sin." And having "returned to the shepherd and guardian of [our] souls," we can with confidence, as Psalm 23 states, "walk in the dark valley" and "fear no evil."

Scripture: Acts 2:14a, 36–41; Psalm 23:1–3a, 3b–4, 5, 6; 1 Peter 2:20b–25; John 10:1–10

FIFTH SUNDAY OF EASTER

If I go and prepare a place for you, I will come back again and take you to myself, so that where I am you also may be. (John 14:3)

The Bridegroom Is Preparing a Place for His Bride

This Sunday's gospel reading is jam-packed with profound Trinitarian theology: "If you know me, then you will also know the Father." "I am in the Father and the Father is in me." "The Father who dwells in me is doing his works." Each of these passages speaks to the eternal bond of love between the Father and the Son that *is* the Holy Spirit. The gospel also tells of how our participation in the life of the Trinity is the fulfillment of human desire and how all of this is revealed through the human body. Participation in this eternal exchange of love and bliss is the North Pole to which the compass of human desire points. Christ came precisely to lead us to the eternal bliss and love that flows from the Father: "Master, show us the Father, and that will be enough for us," says Philip. *Enough* is a word that speaks to fulfillment. How do we *see* the Father and thus attain that which is *enough* for us? The *body* of Christ reveals the mystery: "Whoever has seen me has seen the Father." Christ has gone ahead of us to prepare a place for us. To Jewish ears, this was all nuptial or marital. In Jewish culture, the bridegroom prepared a place for his bride in his father's house. Faith cries out with the Spirit and the Bride, "Come, Lord Jesus! Come and take your Bride home to be with you forever!"

Scripture: Acts 6:1–7; Psalm 33:1–2, 4–5, 18–19; 1 Peter 2:4–9; John 14:1–12

SIXTH SUNDAY
OF EASTER

*Always be ready to give an explanation to anyone who
asks you for a reason for your hope. (1 Peter 3:15b)*

The Hope and Joy of Eros Fulfilled in the
Marriage of the Lamb

In this Sunday's second reading, St. Peter exhorts us to be
always ready to explain the reason for our hope. The *Catechism of the Catholic Church* says that hope is the virtue
"that responds to the aspiration to happiness which God
has placed in the heart of every man" (1818). The Greeks
called that *eros,* and the Church has adopted that language
to describe our yearning for the Infinite, for God. Tragically,
we often make the mistake of aiming eros at finite pleasures
(God substitutes), expecting them to be our satisfaction.
When we do so, we sin; to use an archer's term, we "miss the
mark." *Destiny* is another archer's term. It means "to aim at."
St. John Paul II observed that "hope turns us toward God
as the aim." The virtue of hope, if we let it, the *Catechism*
goes on to teach, purifies our desires "so as to order them
to the Kingdom of heaven," opening our hearts "in expec-
tation of eternal beatitude." We are created for bliss. We

are created for ecstasy. We are created for the fulfillment of eros in the eternal embrace of divinity and humanity in the "Marriage of the Lamb." The more we let this hope sink in, the more we will experience the sentiment of the responsorial psalm—"Let all the earth cry out to God with joy!"—into our lives.

Scripture: Acts 8:5–8, 14–17; Psalm 66:1–3, 4–5, 6–7, 16, 20; 1 Peter 3:15–18; John 14:15–21

THE ASCENSION OF THE LORD

May the eyes of your hearts be enlightened,
that you may know what is the hope that belongs to his call,
what are the riches of glory in his inheritance among the holy
ones. (Ephesians 1:18)

Christ's Bodily Ascension and the Riches of Glory That Await Us

The first reading marking the Ascension of the Lord, celebrated either forty days after Easter or on the seventh Sunday of Easter, tells us that Jesus "was lifted up, and a cloud took him from their sight." In the psalm we respond, "God mounts his throne to shouts of joy: a blaze of trumpets for the Lord." But it's in the second reading, from Ephesians, that we see what this actually has to do with our own lives. Christ's *bodily* Ascension into heaven reveals "the hope that belongs to his call." The hope is this: the humanity that we all share has entered eternal bliss, body and soul, and this means we now "have confidence that we too shall go where [Christ] has preceded us" (CCC 661). The Church is so often accused of "demonizing" the body. This is not so! Demons demonize the body and then blame the Church for their dirty work. Through the bodily Ascension of Christ into heaven, the Church proclaims the "divinization" of the body. Christ's bodily Ascension into heaven indicates "the irreversible entry of his humanity into divine glory" (CCC 659). That is where following Christ leads. "May the eyes of [our] hearts be enlightened," as St. Paul exhorts us in the second reading, that we may know "what are the riches of glory" that await us as followers of the Lord.

Scripture: Acts 1:1–11; Psalm 47:2–3, 6–7, 8–9; Ephesians 1:17–23; Matthew 28:16–20

SEVENTH SUNDAY OF EASTER

Now this is eternal life, that they should know you, the only true God . . . (John 17:3)

To See Within the Temple

The late Monsignor Luigi Giusanni wrote: "Life is hunger, thirst, and passion for an ultimate object, which looms over the horizon, yet always lies beyond it. When this is recognized, man becomes a tireless searcher." The psalmist expresses the ultimate object of his desire this way: "One thing I ask of the LORD; this I seek: to dwell in the house of the LORD all the days of my life, that I may gaze on the loveliness of the LORD and contemplate his temple" (Ps 27:4). Human life, right from its origins, is a mystery of indwelling, as we are all conceived and dwell within our mother's womb. This is our initial home, but it's only a shadow of our eternal indwelling in the house of the Lord. And mystery of mysteries: at the heart of the Christian claim is the declaration that woman's womb has, in fact, become the dwelling place of the Lord. Based on its roots, "to contemplate" means "to see within the temple." We long to contemplate Mary, to see the beauty of the Lord *within her*. Is this not, in the final analysis, the one thing we all long for—to gaze on the beauty of the living God within the womb of Mary, to *know* the divine life conceived within her, to dwell there immersed forever in the beauty and mystery of it all, and, thus, to experience an eternal homecoming? "Now this is eternal life," says Jesus in today's gospel, "that they should know you, the only true God, and Jesus Christ, whom you have sent" (Jn 17:3). Let us respond with the faith of the psalmist: "I believe that I shall see the good things of the Lord in the land of the living."

Scripture: Acts 1:12–14; Psalm 27:1, 4, 7–8; 1 Peter 4:13–16; John 17:1–11a

PENTECOST SUNDAY

Then there appeared to them tongues as of fire,
which parted and came to rest on each one of them.
And they were all filled with the Holy Spirit
and began to speak in different tongues, as the
Spirit enabled them to proclaim. (Acts 2:3–4)

Spirit and Body Together at Pentecost

What does it mean to be "filled with the Holy Spirit," as the first reading on the Feast of Pentecost proclaims? And what does this have to do with our bodies? The Holy Spirit is the "personal love" exchanged eternally between Father and Son. Pentecost celebrates the utterly astounding fact that we now participate in that same exchange: "The personal relation of the Son to the Father is something that man cannot conceive of nor the angelic powers even dimly see: and yet, the Spirit of the Son grants a participation in that very relation to us who believe that Jesus is the Christ and that we are born of God" (CCC 2780). Our bodies tell us that story: the life-giving communion of husband and wife is "a sign of the communion of the Father and the Son in the Holy Spirit" (CCC 2205). Our bodies participate in *this* glory: Pentecost is not so much the *descent* of the Spirit on us as it is the proof that our humanity—body and soul— has *ascended* in Christ into the eternal exchange of Father and Son, which is the Holy Spirit.

Scripture: Acts 2:1–11; Psalm 104:1, 24, 29–30, 31, 34; 1 Corinthians 12:3b–7, 12–13; John 20:19–23

SOLEMNITY OF THE MOST HOLY TRINITY

*The grace of the Lord Jesus Christ and the love of God
and the fellowship of the Holy Spirit be with all of you.*
(2 Corinthians 13:13)

Celebrating the Trinity

What *is* the "grace" and "love" and "fellowship" into which we
are invited in today's second reading? To recognize God as
Trinity is to recognize God as perfect, blissful "love-as-com-
munion." And that means a love eternally poured out by
the One who is love's originator, eternally received by the
Beloved and eternally returned to the One who originally
poured it out. And then eternally poured out again and
again. The one who "pours out" is the Father, the one who
"receives" is the Son, and the eternal "procession" of love
between them is the Holy Spirit. Recall that our bodies
tell *this* story: the life-giving communion of husband and
wife is "a sign and image of the communion of the Father
and the Son in the Holy Spirit" (CCC 2205). This is what
makes our bodies not only biological but also theological.
St. Paul, pray for us that we might embrace this "grace of the
Lord Jesus Christ and the love of God and the fellowship of

the Holy Spirit." Pray for us that we might keep this grace close to our hearts and live out the theology of our bodies.

Scripture: Exodus 34:4b–6, 8–9; Daniel 3:52, 53, 54, 55, 56; 2 Corinthians 13:11–13; John 3:16–18

SOLEMNITY OF THE MOST HOLY BODY AND BLOOD OF CHRIST (CORPUS CHRISTI)

Amen, amen, I say to you, unless you eat the flesh of the Son of Man and drink his blood, you do not have life within you. . . . Whoever eats my flesh and drinks my blood remains in me and I in him.
(John 6:53, 56)

Feasting on Christ's Body

Today as the Church celebrates Corpus Christi Sunday, the "Solemnity of the Most Holy Body and Blood of Christ," it proclaims (as it does at every Mass) the "spousal mystery" of divine love revealed through the theology of our bodies.

The Eucharist is "the Sacrament of the Bridegroom and of the Bride," wrote St. John Paul II in his apostolic letter *Mulieris Dignitatem*. In the Eucharist, "Christ is united with his 'body' as the bridegroom with the bride" (26). In this light, the following line from today's gospel becomes beautifully illuminated: "Amen, Amen, I say to you, unless you eat the flesh of the Son of Man and drink his blood, you do not have life within you." That's like saying, "Unless a bride be in union with her bridegroom, she cannot conceive." When we understand how our own bodies as male and female proclaim this "great mystery" (see Ephesians 5:31–32), *all* the more difficult teachings of the Church begin to make complete and beautiful sense. Lord, through the gift of Christ's Body, give us eyes to see the theology of our own bodies. Amen.

Scripture: Deuteronomy 8:2–3, 14b–16a; Psalm 147:12–13, 14–15, 19–20; 1 Corinthians 10:16–17; John 6:51–58

SOLEMNITY OF SAINTS PETER AND PAUL, APOSTLES

But who do you say that I am? (Matthew 16:15)

Son of Man and Son of God

In the gospel for the Solemnity of Saints Peter and Paul, Apostles, Jesus asks his disciples, "Who do people say that the Son of Man is?" Peter responds, "You are the Son of the living God." What a juxtaposition! We have Jesus, who is God, declaring himself "Son of Man," and we have a man declaring Jesus "Son of God." He is, of course, *both*: fully God and fully man. He is in himself the marriage of the human and the divine, a marriage that is consummated in the "bridal chamber" of Mary's womb. As St. John Paul II wrote in his extended catechesis on the Blessed Mother, Mary offered "the Lord the true heart of a bride. . . . At the moment of the Annunciation, she responded to the proposal of divine love with her own spousal love." At the precise time that Peter proclaimed Jesus "Son of the living God," he too had his own kind of "annunciation." For "no one can say 'Jesus is Lord' except by the holy Spirit" (1 Cor 12:3). Today, Jesus is asking us who we say he is. Before we answer, let us follow Mary and Peter's lead and open ourselves, like a Bride, to the power of God's Spirit.

Scripture: Acts 12:1–11; Psalm 34:2–3, 4–5, 6–7, 8–9; 2 Timothy 4:6–8, 17–18; Matthew 16:13–19

ORDINARY TIME

NINTH SUNDAY
IN ORDINARY TIME

All have sinned and are deprived of the glory of God.
(Romans 3:23)

Desiring What We Really Desire

We are made to participate in God's infinite glory through
the eternal marriage of Christ and the Church. It's our ultimate destiny and our deepest yearning. Yet St. Paul tells
us in today's second reading that "all have sinned and are
deprived of the glory of God" (Rom 3:23). This is what sin
does: it deprives us of the satisfaction of our deepest yearning. It's not merely the breaking of a law; it's the aiming of
our desire for infinite glory at "false infinities," to use Pope
Benedict XVI's expression. Salvation from sin, therefore,
means redirecting our desires towards what we really desire:
the glory of the eternal nuptials of heaven and earth. It is a
terrible blasphemy to reduce the Gospel to a list of rules to
follow. Yet, tragically, many people have been raised in the
Church with just such a truncated vision of things. In turn,
they are condemned to a life of futilely trying to follow God's
law in order to "win" his approval. St. Paul boldly proclaims
that "a person is justified by faith apart from works of the

law" (Rom 3:28). As the *Catechism* says, "The Law of the Gospel . . . does not add new external precepts, but proceeds to reform the heart, the root of human acts, where man chooses between the pure and the impure" (CCC 1968). Or, we could say that the Gospel redirects the heart towards the glory of God, towards true infinity. Allowing our hearts to be reformed in this way, we become "like a wise man who built his house on rock" (Mt 7:24).

Scripture: Deuteronomy 11:18, 26–28, 32; Psalm 31:2–3a, 3b–4, 17, 25; Romans 3:21–25, 28; Matthew 7:21–27

TENTH SUNDAY IN ORDINARY TIME

He will come to us . . . like spring rain that waters the earth.
(Hosea 6:3)

Let Us Strive to Know the Lord

In today's first reading the prophet Hosea exhorts us: "Let us know, let us strive to know the Lord" (6:3). St. John Paul II comments that this "knowledge" harkens back to the conjugal union of Adam who "knew" his wife, Eve, and she bore a son (see Gn 4:1). In this way Hosea places us within the great spousal analogy of the scriptures (see TOB 22: footnote 32). Hints of this same spousal imagery can be seen in the next line of Hosea: "He will come to us like the rain, like spring rain that waters the earth" (6:3). Rain falls from heaven and makes the earth fertile. In turn, the life-givingness of the earth speaks of the life-givingness of God. Furthermore, the life-givingness of creation culminates in that biblical "knowledge" that brings new human life into the world. Today's second reading also speaks of how God's covenant of love is revealed through fruitful nuptial union: Abraham "believed, hoping against hope, that he would become 'the father of many nations'" (Rom 4:18). Then St. Paul compares Abraham's faith in God's ability to bring life from a "dead womb" to Christian faith in God's ability to bring life from a dead tomb (see Romans 4:24). In all of this we can see, as St. John Paul II wrote, how it is possible to explain "spiritual and supernatural [realities] through the likeness of the body and of the love by which . . . husband and wife become 'one flesh'" (TOB 92:3). We must always remember that the body is not only biological; it is also theological. Lord, open our eyes to the divine mysteries our bodies proclaim!

Scripture: Hosea 6:3–6; Psalm 50:1, 8, 12–13, 14–15; Romans 4:18–25; Matthew 9:9–13

ELEVENTH SUNDAY IN ORDINARY TIME

We were reconciled to God through the death of his Son . . .
(Romans 5:10)

The "Mad Eros" of God

In the first reading, God exorts the Israelites: "If you hearken to my voice and keep my covenant, you shall be my special possession, dearer to me than all other people, though all the earth is mine" (Ex 19:5). God, as God, already has claim over everything. And yet, as the *Catechism* says, "God does not want to impose the good, but wants free beings" (CCC 2847, quoting Origen). If heaven is going to be the wedding of Christ and the Church, we can say for certain that it is not going to be a shotgun wedding. God respects our freedom. He wants us to enter this covenant of love freely, otherwise it wouldn't be a covenatnt of love. Tragically, we have been the unfaithful party in this marriage. We've taken our yearning for infinite love (eros) to lovers other than God. The good news as proclaimed by St. Paul in today's second reading is that "we were reconciled to God through the death of his Son" (Rom 5:10). "On the Cross, God's eros for us is made manifest," says Pope Benedict

XVI. "Eros is indeed . . . that force which 'does not allow the lover to remain in himself but moves him to become one with the beloved.' Is there more 'mad eros' . . . than that which led the Son of God to make himself one with us even to the point of suffering as his own the consequences of our offences?" Lord, teach us how to open our hearts to your "mad eros." Let us not fear to catch this divine fire!

Scripture: Exodus 19:2–6a; Psalm 100:1–2, 3, 5; Romans 5:6–11; Matthew 9:36–10:8

TWELFTH SUNDAY IN ORDINARY TIME

Adam . . . is the type of the one who was to come.
(Romans 5:14)

Christ Makes Our Supreme Calling Clear

In today's second reading, St. Paul tells us that Adam is a type, or foreshadowing, of Christ. And, as the Church has always understood these truths, Adam cannot be understood apart from Eve, just as Christ cannot be understood apart from the Church. This means that right from the beginning the original communion of man and woman in "one flesh" was a foreshadowing of the definitive communion of Christ with his bride, the Church. As the Second Vatican Council proclaimed: "The truth is that only in the mystery of the incarnate Word does the mystery of man take on light. For Adam, the first man, was a figure of him who was to come, namely Christ the Lord" (*Gaudium et Spes* 22). This means that the Incarnation is not "plan B." It was already inherent in God's original plan before sin entered the world. For God's plan from all eternity is that Christ would become one in the flesh with his bride, the Church. In fact, St. John Paul II wrote that man already experienced this "supernatural endowment" *before sin* and that this original gift "was brought about precisely *out of regard for [Christ]* ... while chronologically anticipating his coming in the body" (TOB 96:5). Of course, through original sin, the first man and woman forfeited this divine gift. "Redemption was to become the source of man's supernatural endowment after sin and, in a certain sense, despite sin" (TOB 96:5). It is through this gift of our redemption that "Christ, the final Adam ... fully reveals man to man himself and makes his supreme calling clear" (*Gaudium et Spes* 22). What is that supreme calling? Eternal bliss within the life of the Trinity through the fact that we have become "one flesh" with Christ. This is the grace of God that overflows for the many (see Romans 5:15).

Scripture: Jeremiah 20:10–13; Psalm 69:8–10, 14, 17, 33–35; Romans 5:12–15; Matthew 10:26–33

THIRTEENTH SUNDAY IN ORDINARY TIME

If, then, we have died with Christ, we believe that we shall also live with him. (Romans 6:8)

Born to a New and Immortal Life

In today's second reading, St. Paul writes: "We were indeed buried with him through baptism into death, so that, just as Christ was raised from the dead . . . we too might live in newness of life" (Rom 6:4). This newness of life comes about through newness of birth, through supernatural regeneration. St. John Paul II wrote that Baptism is *"the expression of [Christ's] spousal love"* (TOB 91:7). In and through Baptism, Christ pours his spousal love out upon his Bride, the Church, and she "brings forth sons, who are conceived by the Holy Spirit and born of God, to a new and immortal life" (CCC 507). In this way we see that Baptism is a "nuptial mystery" (1617) "in which the 'imperishable seed' of the Word of God produces its life-giving effect" (1228). Our natural father and mother provide an invaluable service in cooperating with God in generating our natural life. And, if we are parents ourselves, what an honor it is to have been chosen to generate children in union with God. However, as Christ points out in today's gospel, these natural family relationships are not our be all and end all: "Whoever loves father or mother more than me is not worthy of me, and whoever loves son or daughter more than me is not worthy of me" (Mt 10:37). Baptism is the entryway into the new dimension of grace, which, building on nature, takes us into a supernatural set of familial relationships. If we cling to our lives as we know them, Christ says we'll lose them. But if we lose our lives for Christ's sake, we'll find something beyond what nature dares to dream or imagine. Lord, open our hearts to these supernatural family relationships. May we not cling to the here and now, but live in joyful hope of what awaits us in the hereafter.

Scripture: 2 Kings 4:8–11, 14–16a; Psalm 89:2–3, 16–17, 18–19; Romans 6:3–4, 8–11; Matthew 10:37–42

FOURTEENTH SUNDAY IN ORDINARY TIME

You are not in the flesh; on the contrary, you are in the spirit, if only the Spirit of God dwells in you.
(Romans 8:9)

Redemption of the Flesh

In the second reading, St. Paul contrasts living "according to the flesh" with living "according to the Spirit." Read out of context, it can seem as though St. Paul is condemning the body as something evil. Let us remember, however, that it's impossible for the Bible to have heresy in it, and the idea that our bodies are evil is exactly that. When St. Paul calls us to live "according to the Spirit," he is not saying we should reject our bodies. Rather, he's inviting us to *open* our bodies to the indwelling of the Holy Spirit. What happens when we do that? "If the Spirit of the one who raised Jesus from the dead dwells in you, the one who raised Christ from the dead will give life to your mortal bodies also, through his Spirit that dwells in you" (Rom 8:11). It is certainly true, as Paul tells us, that flesh ends in death. My body and your body are headed for the grave. But that's not the final word. For "we believe in the Word made flesh in order to redeem the flesh; we believe in the resurrection of the flesh, the fulfillment of both the creation and the redemption of the flesh" (CCC 1015).

Scripture: Zechariah 9:9–10; Psalm 145:1–2, 8–9, 10–11, 13–14; Romans 8:9, 11–13; Matthew 11:25–30

FIFTEENTH SUNDAY IN ORDINARY TIME

So shall my word be that goes forth from my mouth;
my word shall not return to me void, but shall do my will,
achieving the end for which I sent it. (Isaiah 55:11)

The Land Shall Be Espoused

"Your land shall be espoused," says the prophet Isaiah. Keep in mind that "land," like "earth" and "creation," symbolizes the "Bride" (Israel/Church) in scripture. Now reread these passages: "Just as from the heavens the rain and snow come down ... making [the earth] fertile ... so shall my word be." The responsorial psalm tells us that the "Lord has prepared the land: drenching its furrows ... blessing its yield." From the second reading we "know that all creation is groaning in labor pains . . . we also groan within ourselves as we wait for . . . the redemption of our bodies." Now think about these words from the gospel: "Some seed fell on rich soil, and produced fruit." Do you see the "spousal mystery"? Creation is "giving birth" (groaning in labor pains) because the Creator-Bridegroom has given his "imperishable seed" (see 1 Peter 1:23) to his creation-bride. And *all* is fulfilled in Mary. She's the "good soil" that received heaven's seed, heaven's rain, and heaven's word. Mary is the apex of all created fertility. Every seed that falls in the ground and blossoms into life points to the Annunciation. Mary, teach us how to be "good soil" that remains ever open to God's infinitely good seed.

Scripture: Isaiah 55:10–11; Psalm 65:10, 11, 12–13, 14; Romans 8:18–23; Matthew 13:1–23

SIXTEENTH SUNDAY IN ORDINARY TIME

He who sows good seed is the Son of Man, the field is the world, the good seed the children of the kingdom.
(Matthew 13:37–38a)

Fertility and the Battle between Good and Evil

This Sunday's readings continue with the same themes and language from a week ago: seed, soil, and groaning. Speaking in spousal categories, *seed* refers to the Bridegroom, *soil* to the Bride. When seed and soil meet, new life springs forth, and that entails *groaning*. Why? Right from the first pages of Genesis, we discover that *fertility* places us in a raging battle between good and evil: "I will put enmity between you and the woman and between your offspring and hers" (3:15). Mary is the woman; Jesus is her seed. The enemy is Satan. The enemy's hatred ("enmity") is aimed at "the woman" and her ability to bear offspring. "He who sows good seed is the Son of Man. . . . The weeds are the children of the evil one, and the enemy who sows them is the devil." We win this battle by remaining always open (like Mary) to the "good seed" and not being deceived by the bad. But how can we know the difference? We are so weak and the enemy so cunning. St. Paul reminds us that the "Spirit comes to the aid of our weakness; for we do not know how to pray as we ought, but the Spirit itself intercedes with inexpressible groanings . . . according to God's will." Lord, may your will be done in us.

Scripture: Wisdom 12:13, 16–19; Psalm 86:5–6, 9–10, 15–16; Romans 8:26–27; Matthew 13:24–43

SEVENTEENTH SUNDAY IN ORDINARY TIME

The kingdom of heaven is like a treasure buried in a field. (Matthew 13:44a)

The Treasure and the Field

For a few weeks now we've been reflecting in the Sunday readings on the "earth," the "land," and the "soil" as symbols of the "Bride." Ultimately they are all symbols of Mary. The same theme continues in this week's gospel: The person who finds the buried treasure in the field "goes and sells all that he has and buys that field." He does this out of joy. The "treasure" of course is Jesus. And the "field" is Mary. To get the treasure, the person in the parable *had* to buy the field. You can't have Jesus without Mary as you can't have Adam without Eve. The first and the second *always* go together. Jesus and Mary have always been indissolubly united by God. "If, then, it is impossible to separate what God has united," wrote St. Pius X, "it is also certain that you cannot find Jesus except with Mary and through Mary." And St. Louis de Montfort said, "It would be easier to separate the light from the sun than Mary from Jesus." God comes to us through woman. This is the glory of the female body. In

Mary the female body has become the dwelling place of the Most High God. Let us "sell everything" to have Mary. And in having her, we'll have the divine treasure within.

Scripture: 1 Kings 3:5, 7–12; Psalm 119:57, 72, 76–77, 127–128, 129–130; Romans 8:28–30; Matthew 13:44–52

EIGHTEENTH SUNDAY IN ORDINARY TIME

You open your hand and satisfy the desire of every living thing. (Psalm 145:16)

Satisfaction of Our Deepest Desires

Do we really believe the response to this week's Psalm? "The hand of the Lord feeds us; he answers all our needs." Christ's entire mission is to save us from the lie that to satisfy our fundamental hunger (what the Greeks called *eros*) is up to us. And to what length he goes! Christ comes as finest wheat to be ground into flour and baked into bread for us to eat until satisfied. He comes as the juiciest grapes to be crushed in the winepress so we might drink his gift until intoxicated. "All you who are thirsty, come . . . without paying and without cost, drink wine and milk!" says the prophet Isaiah. And in the feeding of the five thousand from the gospel, we're assured that "all ate and were satisfied." Why, then, do we spend "money for what is not bread . . . for what fails to satisfy"? "Follow me," the Lord insists, "and you shall . . . delight in rich fare." Are we willing, truly willing, to entrust the deepest hungers of our hearts to the Lord? When we are tempted to take satisfaction into our own hands, let us instead pray, "Into your hands, Lord, I commend the satisfaction of my every desire." That prayer will save us from a multitude of sins.

Scripture: Isaiah 55:1–3; Psalm 145:8–9, 15–16, 17–18; Romans 8:35, 37–39; Matthew 14:13–21

NINETEENTH SUNDAY IN ORDINARY TIME

During the fourth watch of the night, he came toward them walking on the sea. (Matthew 14:25)

Seeing Human Bodies Doing Things beyond Nature

Seeing Jesus walking toward them on the water, the disciples cry out in fear, "It is a ghost!" This calls to mind a later scene in the gospel when the resurrected Christ appears to the disciples in the upper room and "they were startled and terrified and thought that they were seeing a ghost" (Lk 24:37). In both cases the disciples see a human body doing something beyond its nature. Hence, they conclude (understandably) that what they are seeing is *not* a human body. But *au contraire*, it *is*! This is what is absolutely astounding about the Christian faith and what sets it apart from all other religions: *it immortalizes and divinizes the body*. By uniting his divine nature to our human nature, Christ takes the human body beyond nature. And he invites us to join him: "Come," he said to Peter. And Peter, with his eyes fixed on Christ, got out of the boat and walked on water—until his faith wavered. Where does our faith in God's power to take our bodies "beyond nature" waiver? We do believe, Lord. Help our unbelief.

Scripture: 1 Kings 19:9a, 11–13a; Psalm 85:9ab, 10, 11–12, 13–14; Romans 9:1–5; Matthew 14:22–33

TWENTIETH SUNDAY IN ORDINARY TIME

Then Jesus said to her in reply,
"O woman, great is your faith!" (Matthew 15:28a)

A Unity in Distinction

The common theme in each of the readings this weekend is the unity of Jew and Gentile in God's plan of salvation. As with all true unities, however, it is a unity in distinction. Jesus drives this point home in a rather dramatic way in his treatment of the Canaanite woman who pleads for his help. Jesus first states that he was sent only to the lost sheep of Israel, even comparing this Canaanite to a "dog" that shouldn't get the food of the children of Israel. Yikes! Is Jesus really so insulting and heartless? Impossible. He's testing her. And we have much to learn from her persistence. Jesus assures her she's passed the test when he calls her "woman"—a term of deep love and affection that takes us back to Genesis and the joy that Adam took in beholding his bride, calling her "woman." There is a distinction between Jew and Gentile, just as there is between man and woman. These distinctions should never be blurred, for it is precisely these distinctions that enable a true unity. Only in this light can we understand St. Paul's teaching that there is neither Jew nor Gentile, male or female, for all are "one in Christ Jesus" (Gal 3:28).

Scripture: Isaiah 56:1, 6–7; Psalm 67:2–3, 5, 6, 8; Romans 11:13–15, 29–32; Matthew 15:21–28

TWENTY-FIRST SUNDAY IN ORDINARY TIME

Blessed are you, Simon son of Jonah. For flesh and blood has not revealed this to you, but my heavenly Father. (Matthew 16:17)

Flesh and Blood in Communion with God

Christ intentionally contrasts "flesh and blood" with his "heavenly Father." What he is doing is contrasting God with humanity. This contrast opens the way to the astounding truth of God's plan for reconciling the world to himself. In fact, the eternal "Son of the living God" has taken on "flesh and blood." And *that* is who is standing before Peter. "Flesh and blood" is now welcomed into eternal communion with the heavenly Father. This is the depth of what Peter realized in calling Jesus "Son of the living God." In Christ, Simon is no longer merely "son of Jonah." Peter, too, can become a son of the heavenly Father, an heir to glory and bliss beyond all telling. And so can we. Astounding!

Scripture: Isaiah 22:19–23; Psalm 138:1–2a, 2b–3, 6, 8; Romans 11:33–36; Matthew 16:13–20

TWENTY-SECOND SUNDAY IN ORDINARY TIME

My soul is thirsting for you, O Lord my God.
(Psalm 63:2b)

Our Flesh Pines for the Lord

The Psalm for this Sunday's Mass speaks of deep, aching *desire* for the Lord: "For you my flesh pines and my soul thirsts." Pope Benedict XVI adds, "Not only my soul, but even every fiber of my flesh is made to find . . . fulfillment in God." Even when we try to run from God, as did the prophet Jeremiah, "it becomes like fire burning in my heart." Yes, whatever a person might do, the desire for the Infinite remains in humanity, says Benedict XVI, "like a signature imprinted with fire in his soul and body by the Creator himself." What are we to do when our bodies are burning up with desire and crying out for satisfaction? Right in those moments when we are most tempted to take satisfaction into our own hands, we must instead "offer our bodies as a living sacrifice" to God, as St. Paul tells us in the second reading. Or as Christ says in the gospel, we must deny ourselves and follow him. And that means entrusting every desire, every cry of our hearts—even as we taste the bitter sufferings of Christ—to the One who alone can fulfill us, and has promised he will.

Scripture: Jeremiah 20:7–9; Psalm 63:2, 3–4, 5–6, 8–9; Romans 12:1–2; Matthew 16:21–27

TWENTY-THIRD SUNDAY IN ORDINARY TIME

For where two or three are gathered together
in my name, there am I in the midst of them.
(Matthew 18:20)

Our Bodies Tell the Story of Love and Communion

Why does Jesus mention "two or three" gathered together in his name? Because two and then three are the basic building blocks of communion. This is how we "fulfill the law," as St. Paul says in this week's second reading: by loving one another. The Church is the embodiment of the call of the whole human race to live in love and communion. And that call to love and communion is revealed most fundamentally in our creation as male and female and the call of the two to become "one flesh." Here, in the normal course of events, the union of the "two" leads to a "third," the organic growth and expansion of human communion. When true human communion grows, without a doubt, Christ is "in the midst of them." Christ's promise to be in our "midst" is all the more telling when we link this with the words of the prophet Zephaniah: "The Lord, your God, is in your midst" (3:17), which literally means "the Lord is in your womb." When we love one another rightly, we "conceive" Christ. Our bodies tell the story.

Scripture: Ezekiel 33:7–9; Psalm 95: 1–2, 6–7, 8–9; Romans 13: 8–10; Matthew 18:15–20.

TWENTY-FOURTH SUNDAY IN ORDINARY TIME

None of us lives for oneself, and no one dies for oneself.
(Romans 14:7)

The Call Out of Ourselves

Experience seems to contradict St. Paul's observation in today's second reading. Don't we all know people who live for themselves? It would appear that the Apostle is exhorting us *not* to live for ourselves but to "live for the Lord" and also to "die for the Lord" (Rom 14:8). Contrary to our basic instinct to avoid thoughts about death, the Bible has repeated admonitions, like in today's first reading, to "remember death and decay." It should wake us up, and make us "cease from sin" (Sir 27:30), and call us out of ourselves. This call out of ourselves (ex-stasis, or ecstasy) is written right in our bodies. A man's body makes no sense by itself. Nor does a woman's. Seen in light of each other, we discover what St. John Paul II called the spousal meaning of our bodies: that is, we discover the call to be a life-giving gift to the other. Marriage is the paradigmatic way of living the spousal meaning of the body, but it's not the only way to do so. Every time and in every way we make a sincere gift of ourselves to and for others, and also everytime we affirm and receive the gift of another, we are living the spousal meaning of our bodies. And, by doing so, as John Paul II says, we "fulfill the very meaning of [our] being and existence" (TOB 15:1), which is to love as Christ loves. Whether we live or die, we can do so loving as Christ loves; either way, "we are the Lord's," as Paul tells us (see Romans 14:9).

Scripture: Sirach 27:30–28:7; Psalm 103:1–2, 3–4, 9–10, 11–12; Romans 14:7–9; Matthew 18:21–35

FEAST OF THE EXALTATION OF THE HOLY CROSS

And just as Moses lifted up the serpent in the desert,
so must the Son of Man be lifted up, so that everyone
who believes in him may have eternal life. (John 3:14)

Lift High the Marriage Bed of the Cross

This Sunday is the Feast of the Exultation of the Cross. Christ's reference to the Cross—of being lifted up to eternal life—hides within it all the glory of the spousal symbolism of what happened at Calvary. The Cross is where, to use St.

Augustine's famous expression, Christ mounted his "marriage bed" to consummate his union with the Church, his Bride. Where is this hidden in what Christ said above? It is hidden in the fact that the Cross grants us "eternal life." Eternal life is a gift of grace. And grace builds on nature. Hence, to understand how *eternal life* is given, we must look to how *temporal life* is given. That's the model upon which grace builds. Temporal life is given through the union of spouses in "one flesh." This is a "great mystery" St. Paul tells us, and "it refers to Christ and the Church" (Eph 5:31–32). Augustine even says that Christ pours out "spiritual seminal fluid" in the flow of blood and water from his side, enabling us to be "born again." What a great mystery indeed! Lift high the marriage bed of the Cross.

Scripture: Numbers 21:4b–9; Psalm 78:1b–2, 34–35, 36–37, 38; Philemon 2:6–11; John 3:13–17

TWENTY-FIFTH SUNDAY IN ORDINARY TIME

Conduct yourself in a way worthy of the gospel of Christ.
(Philemon 1:27a)

Generosity Is Written into Our Bodies

What is the way worthy of the Gospel that St. Paul describes in today's second reading? The other readings show us. This way of the Gospel is *generosity*. Our God "is generous in forgiving," says Isaiah in the first reading. And the gospel parable about the landowner who pays a full day's wages to the workers who only worked an hour is all about God's generosity: "Are you envious because I am generous?" Since we are made in God's image as male and female, we would expect to see an image of God's generosity written right into our bodies. And, indeed, we do. God made us sexual beings precisely to enable us to image and participate in the lavishness and generosity of his love. Interestingly, have you ever noticed that the word *eros* is at the center of the word *generosity*? Christ "will be magnified in my body," as St. Paul says, whenever you live eros as the generous gift of yourself for others.

Scripture: Isaiah 55:6–9; Psalm 145:2–3, 8–9, 17–18; Philemon 1:20c–24, 27a; Matthew 20:1–16a

TWENTY-SIXTH SUNDAY IN ORDINARY TIME

*Amen, I say to you, tax collectors and prostitutes are
entering the kingdom of God before you. (Matthew 21:31b)*

A Passion for the Kingdom

Jesus has a way of turning people's religious presuppositions
on their head. Jesus' surprising words about who would
be admitted first into the kingdom of God illustrate this.
Theologian Olivier Clement writes, "In the Gospel the very
root of sin is the pretense that we can save ourselves by our
own effort.... The publicans and harlots enter the Kingdom
before the just because they are well aware that they cannot
save themselves." They are well aware that nothing they have
turned to in their passions has brought them satisfaction,
and so in their utter need and poverty they long for the
Infinite and are attracted to Christ. The chief priests and
elders, on the other hand, have suffocated their longing and
need in favor of self-satisfaction in their own self-defined
virtue. There is, indeed, a great divide between a religion
understood as a "keeping of the law" versus that of a "longing for the Infinite." And this is why, as St. Augustine put

it, "he who loses himself in his passion is less lost than he who loses his passion."

Scripture: Ezekiel 28:25–28; Psalm 25:4–5, 6–7, 8–9; Philemon 2:1–11; Matthew 21:28–32

TWENTY-SEVENTH SUNDAY IN ORDINARY TIME

Finally, he sent his son to them, thinking,
"They will respect my son." (Matthew 21:37)

Believe in the Gift

In this Sunday's gospel, Jesus tells the parable of the landowner who leased his vineyard to tenants who later beat and killed his servants. When the landowner's son came, the tenants said to one another, "This is the heir. Come, let us kill him and acquire his inheritance." Contained in that sentiment is the root of every tragedy known to humankind. In his Theology of the Body, St. John Paul II described original sin (the sin from which all horrors flow) as the *questioning*—and, ultimately, the *denial*—of God's gift. From eternity, the Father has bestowed the riches of his love upon the Son as a free gift, and we all yearn to participate in that inheritance. But we have been tricked into believing the utter lie that God is really a tightwad, that he is keeping his gift to himself and doesn't want to fulfill the desires of our heart. We think the only way to get what we want is to participate in the killing of God's Son. Oh the tragic irony: in the very act of trying to take the life we want, the Son is offering it to us freely. "This is my body given up for you," he clearly tells us. Lord, show us the ways we deny your gift. Help us to repent and believe the good news of your gift to us.

Scripture: Isaiah 5:1–7; Psalm 80:9, 12, 13–14, 15–16, 19–20; Philemon 4:6–9; Matthew 21:33–43

TWENTY-EIGHTH SUNDAY IN ORDINARY TIME

On this mountain the Lord of hosts will provide
for all peoples a feast of rich food and choice wines,
juicy, rich food and pure, choice wines. (Isaiah 25:6)

Come Enter the Wedding Feast!

Whereas last week's readings addressed our lack of faith in God to satisfy the deepest hunger of our hearts, this week's readings are all about how God "will fully supply whatever you need" in the "wedding feast." The prophet Isaiah tells us that it is "a feast of rich food and pure, choice wines." And from the responsorial psalm we know to "spread the table before me . . . my cup overflows." When our hope is set on the wedding feast of eternity, says St. Paul, we know in this life "how to live in humble circumstances" without despairing, and we "know also how to live with abundance" without idolizing earthly pleasures. How do we enter this feast? First, we have to respond to the invitation, and second, we must put on the "wedding garment." This is a reference to the "nuptial mystery" of Baptism when we were clothed in white (see CCC 1617). St. John Paul II tells us that Baptism is "the expression of [Christ's] spousal love." It "makes the Church the Bride of Christ" (TOB 91:7). To enter the eternal wedding feast, we must be *clothed* by Christ's spousal love; we must *enter into* it and be *thoroughly transformed* by it. Lord, come clothe us in your spousal love and wash our soiled garments.

Scripture: Isaiah 25:6–10a; Psalm 23:1–3a, 3b–4, 5, 6; Philemon 4:12–14, 19–20; Matthew 22:1–14

TWENTY-NINTH SUNDAY IN ORDINARY TIME

Then repay to Caesar what belongs to Caesar and to God what belongs to God. (Matthew 22:21b)

Repay God with the Gift of Your Body

In the gospel we hear Jesus' well-known response about the requirement of paying taxes to those who showed him a Roman coin with Caesar's image. The deeper question of course is, What belongs to God? The answer: We do. For we bear God's image and inscription. Where? How? Traditionally theologians have said we image God as individuals, through our rational soul. That's true. But St. John Paul II says that *"man became the image of God not only through his own humanity, but also through the communion of persons,* which man and woman form from the very beginning" (TOB 9:3). God himself is an eternal communion of persons, Father, Son, and Holy Spirit. The call to a similar communion is inscribed by God *right in our bodies* as male and female. The body itself is a witness to self-giving love. God took on a body precisely to make a gift of his body for us. Let us repay God by making a gift of our bodies for him.

Scripture: Isaiah 45:1, 4–6; Psalm 96:1, 3, 4–5, 7–8, 9–10;
1 Thessalonians 1:1–5b; Matthew 22:15–21

THIRTIETH SUNDAY IN ORDINARY TIME

*You shall love the Lord, your God, with all your heart,
with all your soul, and with all your mind. . . . You shall
love your neighbor as yourself. (Matthew 22:37, 39b)*

The Body Is a Witness to Love

In this week's gospel, Jesus tells us that the greatest com-
mandment is to love God. The second greatest is to "love
your neighbor as yourself." One of the insights of St. John
Paul II's Theology of the Body is that this call to love is
revealed in our bodies. "This is the body," says John Paul II,
"a witness . . . to love" (TOB 14:4). It is a witness to the love
God has for us, the love we are to have for God, and the love
we are to have for others. How so? It is the body that reveals
the call to become "one flesh." The holy communion of man
and woman is a "great mystery" that reveals how God loves
us in the holy communion of the Eucharist (see Ephesians
5:31–32). God wants to marry us, become "one" with us in

the flesh. "This is my body given for you," says Jesus to his Bride in the Mass. In receiving Christ's body in so intimate a way, we have all we need when Mass is ended to "go and announce the Gospel of the Lord." We have God's body in our body, the source of all love. Astounding.

Scripture: Exodus 22:20–26; Psalm 18:2–3a, 3b–4, 47, 51; 1 Thessalonians 1:5c–10; Matthew 22:34–40

THIRTY-FIRST SUNDAY IN ORDINARY TIME

Call no one on earth your father. (Matthew 23:9)

The Only Father Who Was Not First a Son

When Christ says we should call no one on earth our father, he is not forbidding us to acknowledge human fatherhood. Rather, he is stating, as the *Catechism* puts it, that "no one is father as God is Father" (CCC 239). We can recognize the infinite otherness of God's fatherhood in this fact: the first person of the Trinity is the only Father who was not first a son. "By calling God 'Father,' the language of faith indicates two main things: that God is the first origin of everything and transcendent authority; and that he is at the same time goodness and loving care for all his children." In calling God Father, however, we must "recall that God transcends the human distinction between the sexes. He is neither man nor woman: he is God. He also transcends human fatherhood" (CCC 239). In a world in which many people have had very painful experiences with their earthly fathers (abandonment, domination, absence, cruelties, and various other abuses) it is understandable that we can encounter difficulties in recognizing God as our Father. It's a mistake, however, to view God in light of our earthly fathers. True healing comes as we view our earthly fathers in light of God's fatherhood and extend mercy to our earthly fathers for their failures. As the *Catechism* keenly observes, to understand God as Father "we must humbly cleanse our hearts of certain false images drawn 'from this world' . . . The *purification* of our hearts has to do with paternal or maternal images, stemming from our personal and cultural history, and influencing our relationship with God. God our Father transcends the categories of the created world. To impose our own ideas in this area 'upon him' would be to fabricate idols to adore or pull down. To pray to the Father is to enter into his mystery as he is and as the Son has revealed him to us" (CCC 2779).

Scripture: Malachi 1:14b–2:2b, 8–10; Psalm 131:1, 2, 3; 1 Thessalonians 2:7b–9, 13; Matthew 23:1–12

SOLEMNITY OF ALL SAINTS

We do know that when it is revealed we shall be like him, for we shall see him as he is. (1 John 3:1b)

A Proclamation of Life, Immortality, and Resurrection

Halloween is a curious phenomenon, isn't it? An annual holiday, sanctioned and monitored by local governments all over the country, that celebrates death with a creepy display of ghosts, corpses, headstones, and skeletons. What gives? Where does such a "celebration" come from in the human psyche? Holiday, of course, means holy day. And Halloween means the "eve of all hallows" because it's the evening before one of the holiest days of the liturgical year. Commonly called All Saints Day, this feast is the Church's annual celebration of all those men and women throughout the ages who have overcome death through the power of the Gospel. Overcome death? If this is possible

. . . if this is real . . . it is *utterly* astounding. Halloween proclaims death, mortality, decay. All Saints' Day proclaims life, immortality, resurrection. Contrary to widespread belief, immortality does not simply refer to the soul, to the spiritual aspect of human nature. Man is a unity of body and soul. Hence, as Peter Kreeft insightfully observes, when death separates the two "we have a freak, a monster, an obscenity." He adds: "That is why we are terrified of ghosts and corpses, though both are harmless: they are the obscenely separated aspects of what belongs together as one." And herein, I believe, lies the deepest psychological origins of this macabre carnival right on the eve of the joyous celebration of all those who have overcome death in Christ. By putting ghosts, corpses, headstones, and skeletons right in our face on the eve of the Church's celebration of all those who have overcome death, it seems the horrors of Halloween are basically saying: "*Really?* Has Christ *really* overcome death?" Today, we have the witness of all the saints proclaiming: "Death is not the final word on human life! The final word is *resurrection.*"

Scripture: Revelation 7:2–4, 9–14; Psalm 24:1–2, 3–4, 5–6; 1 John 3: 1–3; Matthew 5:1–12a

THE COMMEMORATION OF ALL THE FAITHFUL DEPARTED (ALL SOULS)

As gold in the furnace, he proved them, and as sacrificial offerings he took them to himself. (Wisdom 3:6)

Feast of All Souls . . . *and* All Bodies

The Church celebrates the Feast of All Souls. It's distinguished from the Feast of All Saints by the fact that most of us do not die as saints and are still in need of purification. Protestant reformers used the image of a dung heap covered by white snow to convey their understanding of what sin has done to us and how Christ saves us. If that's an accurate image, the idea of purgatory makes no sense: once you say yes to Jesus, you're "covered." The Catholic vision is almost the converse: we are white snow that's been covered by dung through sin, and as we give our yes to Jesus, he removes the dung. From this perspective, purification is a journey, and if that journey is not complete at death, it makes sense that it continues. The book of Wisdom says that as "gold in the furnace" God "tried them and found them worthy of himself." On this Feast of All Souls, the Church also wants to remind us of the destiny of the body. Hence the gospel speaks of the final resurrection. "The proper Christian thing," as Pope Benedict XVI once wrote, "is to speak not of the soul's immortality, but of the resurrection of the complete human being [body and soul] and of that alone." So on the Feast of All Souls, let us also remember All Bodies!

Scripture: Wisdom 3:1–9; Psalm 23:1–3a, 3b–4, 5, 6; Romans 5:5–11 (or Romans 6:3–9); John 6:37–40

THIRTY-SECOND SUNDAY IN ORDINARY TIME

My soul thirsts for you, my body pines for you.
(Psalm 63:1)

Eros Is a Longing for the Infinite

Have you ever noticed how the *Catechism of the Catholic Church* begins? "The desire for God is written in the human heart, because man is created by God and for God; and God never ceases to draw man to himself. Only in God will he find the truth and happiness he never stops searching for"(27). We are made for union. It's stamped right in our bodies as male and female. Yet, the cry of eros for union can only be fulfilled in union with God. Today's psalm, as Pope Benedict XVI observed, "helps us to enter into the heart of [the matter]: 'O God, my God, for you I long at break of day; my soul thirsts for you, my body pines for you, like a dry land without water.' Not only my soul, but even every fiber of my flesh is made to find . . . its fulfillment in God. And this tension [eros] cannot be erased from man's heart." Those Christians who take up Christ's invitation to forego marriage "for the sake of the kingdom" (see Matthew 19:12) are not meant to repress eros. Rather, they're meant to aim it at the eternal, showing the rest of the world where ultimate happiness truly lies. Of course, as we learn in today's gospel, we must distinguish between the "wise" and the "unwise" virgins. The unwise have no oil for their lamps. Papal preacher Raniero Cantalamessa observes that if the desires of the heart connected with eros are "systematically denied or repressed" in the name of celibacy, "the result will be double: either one goes on in a tired way, out of a sense of duty, to defend one's image, or more or less licit compensations are sought, to the point of the very painful cases that are afflicting the Church." The wise virgins, on the other hand, have a full supply of oil and their lamps (their hearts) are set *on fire*. They do not repress eros. Rather, they allow their eros to become what it truly is: a pure, burning, wild, aching longing for God.

Scripture: Wisdom 6:12–16; Psalm 63:2, 3–4, 5–6, 7–8; 1 Thessalonians 4:13–18 (longer form) or 1 Thessalonians 4:13–14 (shorter form); Matthew 25:1–13

FEAST OF THE DEDICATION OF THE LATERAN BASILICA IN ROME

His disciples recalled the words of scripture,
"Zeal for your house will consume me." (John 2:17)

Zeal for the Body Consumed the Lord

The gospel tells the astounding story of Jesus making "a whip out of cords" and driving the money changers from the Temple. It was then that the disciples recalled the words of scripture: "Zeal for your house will consume me." As John's gospel and the other readings this week make clear, the zeal that consumed Christ *was for the temple of the body*. St. Paul writes to the Corinthians, "Do you not know that you are the temple of God?" If Christ's demand to "stop making my

Father's house a marketplace" refers to the body, then this gospel provides an image of the holy rage that Christ has toward anything that obscures the holiness of the body and makes it an object for selfish gain. The body is under violent attack in our porn-filled world today, but life-giving water, referred to in the first reading from the book of the prophet Ezekiel, is always flowing from the temple of Christ's body to bring healing and to gladden the "city of God." As dark as it may get, let us trust that Christ will come in his zeal for the body to "cleanse the temple" and all will behold, as the Psalm tells us, "the astounding things he has wrought on earth."

Scripture: Ezekiel 47:1–2, 8–9, 12; Psalm 46:2–3, 5–6, 8–9; 1 Corinthians 3:9c–11, 16–17; John 2:13–22

THIRTY-THIRD SUNDAY IN ORDINARY TIME

Charm is deceptive and beauty fleeting; the woman who fears the LORD is to be praised. (Proverbs 31:30)

Surface-Love versus Heart-Love

The reading from the book of Proverbs provides important insight into the difference between what we might call "surface-love" and "heart-love." Addressed to men, Proverbs presents this just warning: "Charm is deceptive and beauty fleeting; the woman who fears the LORD is to be praised." Our culture today is fixated on the deceptive and the fleeting, molding us to prize a person's outward charm and beauty above all. But this is a failing prize. While it's true that such "surface-love" can mature into a deeper "heart-love," if love stops at outward charm and beauty, it too will be deceptive and fleeting. Only the inner values of the person can sustain a stable relationship. To acquire those inner values, lovers have to learn how to entrust their hearts to one another. They have to learn how to take their walls down, let their masks fall, and entrust their real humanity, warts and all, to each other. The value of a wife who loves her husband in this way is "far beyond pearls," Proverbs tells us. "Her husband, entrusting his heart to her, has an unfailing prize."

Scripture: Proverbs 31:10–13, 19–20, 30–31; Psalm 128:1–2, 3, 4–5; 1 Thessalonians 5:1–6; Matthew 25:14–30

SOLEMNITY OF OUR LORD JESUS CHRIST, KING OF THE UNIVERSE

For I was hungry and you gave me food, I was thirsty and you gave me drink, a stranger and you welcomed me, naked and you clothed me, ill and you cared for me, in prison and you visited me. (Matthew 25:35–36)

Christ the Bridegroom-King

This Sunday is the Feast of Christ the King. It can be difficult for us in the modern world to relate to "king" and "kingdom" imagery. For many, the idea of being under a king is akin to losing our freedom to an overbearing ruler or tyrant. You might remember playing the childhood game King of the Mountain in which the winner lorded it over the losers. But as Pope Benedict XVI reminds us, "The king is Jesus; in him God entered humanity and espoused it to himself." Yes, Jesus is King and Lord, but as such, he is Bridegroom. As St. John Paul II tells us, "In this manner, the absolute of lordship turns out to be the absolute of love." As the Bridegroom-King, Christ reigns by serving, not by being served. And he wants us to reign in the same way. As we learn in the gospel, this is how the King will judge us: only those who loved as he loved will "inherit the kingdom." We also learn in this gospel passage that to serve others is to serve the King. The King identifies so closely with his subjects precisely because, as Bridegroom, he became one with them. Where do we find the love to serve others in this same way? We find it in letting the King serve us.

Scripture: Ezekiel 34:11–12, 15–17; Psalm 23:1–2a, 2b–3, 5–6; 1 Corinthians 15:20–26, 28; Matthew 25:31–46

SUGGESTIONS FOR FURTHER STUDY

- If you have the aptitude, read St. John Paul II's actual text: *Man and Woman He Created: A Theology of the Body* (Pauline, 2006). If you need help with that, read it in conjunction with my extended commentary *Theology of the Body Explained* or my *Theology of the Body for Beginners*. Visit my ministry's website corproject. com, and click on Shop for a full listing of additional resources.
- Explore what other authors and teachers have written about the Theology of the Body. There are so many good resources out there today, each with their own emphases and insights. Do an internet search of "theology of the body resources" to find them.
- If you would like ongoing formation in the Theology of the Body, consider joining a worldwide community of men and women who are learning, living, and sharing the TOB as members of the Cor Project. Visit cormembership.com to learn more.

117

+ Consider taking a five-day immersion course through the Theology of the Body Institute. Learn more at tobinstitute.org.
+ For more in-depth study, consider the Theology of the Body Institute's certification program or the graduate degree programs offered by the Pontifical John Paul II Institute for Studies on Marriage and Family.

Christopher West is cofounder, president, and senior lecturer of the Theology of the Body Institute. His global lecturing, bestselling books, and multiple audio and video programs have made him one of the world's most recognized teachers of TOB.

West is the author of more than a dozen books, including *Theology of the Body Explained*, *Theology of the Body for Beginners*, and *Good News about Sex and Marriage*. His work has been featured in the *New York Times*, on ABC News, MSNBC, and Fox News, and on countless Catholic and evangelical media platforms.

theologyofthebody.com
christopherwest.com

Facebook: cwestofficial
Twitter: @cwestofficial
Instagram: @cwestofficial

THE COR PROJECT

CHRISTOPHER WEST

Follow Christopher West and The Cor Project at:

 @cwestofficial
(ChristopherWestOfficial)

 @CWestTOB

 The Cor Project (channel)

 christopherwestoffical

Receive ongoing formation in St. John Paul II's *Theology of the Body*.
Read Christopher's blog, learn of upcoming events, and sign up to receive
Christopher's emails (Monday–Friday) and other free resources at:

CORPROJECT.COM